GW00865539

DEAR GOD,

WHAT'S ON THE SECOND FLOOR?

Walter Holland

with Walter Holland Jr

Self-published first edition
ELLICOTTVILLE, NY

Walter Holland Jr.
67 Bay State Rd, Apt D
Cambridge MA 02138
wgh@alum.mit.edu

Authors' Note: This is a work of memoir. Conversations have been reconstructed from memory. Bits of this book are almost certainly misremembered, mischaracterized, or frivolously reimagined – sometimes all three at once. Can't be helped, really, but reasonable effort has been made to correct such mistakes. Remaining distortions, omissions, or balderdash are unintentional, and for them, the authors apologize.

Book Layout ©2017 BookDesignTemplates.com

Ordering Information:
For additional copies, please contact the publisher or visit our website: whatsonthesecondfloor.com.

Dear God, What's on the Second Floor?/
Walter Holland Sr & Walter Holland Jr. -- 1st ed.
ISBN 978-1722610623

For Cata

This
Is the process whereby pain of the past in its pastness
May be converted into the future tense

Of joy.

ROBERT PENN WARREN
'I AM DREAMING OF A WHITE CHRISTMAS'

Contents

By way of introduction

My name is Wally Holland. My dad was Wally Holland Senior, and my mum's name was Mary.

I was born in Manchester, England in 1934. During the war I was sent to Hurst Green in Lancashire; in the late 1940s I was expelled from school, took up a trade – textiles – joined the British Army on my 18th birthday, and volunteered to go to Korea. I was stationed in Kure, Japan, and never saw combat.

I returned to England and worked in textiles for another decade or so, then started working in bars and cabarets.

In the late 1960s I joined BEA as an airline steward, then worked at sea, in Africa and the Caribbean. I met a wonderful woman named Kathleen in San Juan in the late 1970s, got married, and moved to Texas with our two children. We later moved to a little village in western New York State. I started working as a soccer official for high school and middle school games, and still do.

My wife passed away in 2002.

I'm 84 now, writing this with my eldest son, Wally Jr. He lives in Cambridge, Massachusetts; my youngest son Phillippe lives in Chicago. I've got two wonderful daughters-in-law and three marvelous grandsons.

That's a life, isn't it? It's hardly flashy but it's a good life, I think. If that were all, it would be enough.

Lucky for me, that isn't all.

I've been held at gunpoint by a lovesick Australian, threatened at knifepoint by gangsters in a London house of ill repute, and arrested by Interpol in Paris on suspicion of murder.

I've slapped a sergeant, dodged a bullet on the train to Wigan (and bomb scares on a couple of continents), and had an unscheduled rendezvous with a belly dancer. I've played Victor Velasco onstage and Scrooge on the radio. I was in a movie with Alan Ladd, though I like to think *he* was in a movie with *me*.

I was wing-half for an unbeaten soccer team – 31 wins on the trot – and I'm now the oldest soccer official in New York State.

I was the last evacuee to return home from Hurst Green, and once had an excited but silent conversation with James Bond at an airport in London...one of the James Bonds, anyhow. (There are so many of them now.)

I've been frog-marched by the police past not one but *two* girlfriends on the same day, spent the afternoon with the Defense Minister of South Korea (though I like to think *he* spent the afternoon with *me*), and married a woman who deserved me *and* could afford me. I've made the best friends, and had the best times, and settled – quite by accident – in the loveliest place I can imagine.

I'd like to tell you about it, if I may.

CHAPTER 1

A decent beginning

I was born in Hulme, Manchester on the 8th of April 1934, not that you asked.

This is an unusual feeling, what I'm doing now – everyone flashes back sometimes to meeting so-and-so, arriving or leaving someplace. Specific incidents from long ago. But to try to put it all together, to make *sense* of it...it's strange to say, but I've never done that before, never needed to. There's so much to a life, even mine, and for the longest time it seemed as if it was lost – I didn't think I'd ever tell these stories properly. But here we are, and it all begins to come back to me.

I remember Mr Lavin and a beautiful dark-haired lady, teachers of mine when I was perhaps six years old. Mr Lavin offered me a penny if I'd stop asking questions – and I did win the penny, but I know from the memory that I must have chatted too much. That memory teaches me something about myself, and with that in mind, I start to remember other things, to learn from *them*...

A penny was a lot of money to me. I was six years old! The meaning was clear: *Shut up, Wally.*

But I did get the penny.

Mind you, it wasn't so much *chatting* – I'm inquisitive. I do wonder about things. Later on I had a habit of asking my teacher at Cavendish so many questions, what things meant. It's always better to ask; that's what teachers are for. But at some point I must have upset him, maybe embarrassed him or something, because he put three rulers together and hit me on my knuckles. My hands swelled up terribly.

And then a funny thing happened: the big lads in the class at that time surrounded him at his desk. I think they were thinking of giving him a punch for what he'd done to me.

Mr Callahan was the headmaster at Cavendish school: a big-bellied man, Irish obviously, in a suit with a waistcoat, which the Americans call a 'vest.' When I was expelled years later, he made a big speech about me being 'the master forger.' He made a big fuss and asked, —Should we keep him here?!

It was Easter, and he was wondering whether to keep me on at school. And he decided to let me go. Happy Easter, Mr Callahan.

Ten years passed between those two days, Mr Lavin's penny and Mr Callahan's speech, but for me they're both just as far away, or as close by.

When I think back on these things, it's hard – that's a lot of years to cover. Thinking back on yesterday you might say, 'It was like today, only I had a blue suit on.' But to remember 1940 – it was another world entirely, and in so many ways I was a different person. It's near and far away all at once.

I remember once, as a boy, laughing so much that Dad got angry at me. I think he'd hurt himself or something, and I knew it was wrong, but I couldn't stop laughing all the same. He said, —Shut up, you bleeding lunatic!

But I couldn't stop. Poor Dad.

Still, I won the penny from Mr Lavin, so I wasn't completely hopeless.

My mum and dad were both Irish, but I never knew my Irish relatives, only heard about them. I met my mother's parents once, Mr and Mrs O'Riley, at their council house in Ancoats. I was four. And I knew my dad's brothers Albert and Teddy, of course. I don't know when their families came over from Ireland. They didn't keep the same sorts of records in those days. Nowadays you'd have pictures, papers, movies – yesterday my eldest son turned off my television using his computer from 500 miles away, which was good of him.

I'm not even sure where my dad was born. I was told we were the O'Hallorans from County Cork, and it was changed to 'Holland' when we came over. And I want to say my mum was from County Kerry, and had two sisters and a brother. But who knows? Cousin Amy's the one who told me about the changed name and I believe her. I don't mind you buying me a glass of wine on St Patrick's Day if it comes to that.

I must tell you, Mum's name could have been spelled O'Reilly for all I know.

Dad took me to High Street Baths to teach me how to swim. He never succeeded, by the way. Nobody had swim costumes. Do you remember Tarzan, the little thing he wore around his privates? They'd just issue you one of those at the baths. I don't know what the girls wore, since I don't remember the boys and girls ever sharing a pool.

Nowadays, when it's warm I sometimes go to the Holiday Valley pool in Ellicottville; the boys and girls *do* swim together, no harm done. I don't have the Tarzan outfit anymore. You'll be pleased to hear that I replaced it, somewhere along the line, with something more modest.

I can't give you a full picture of Manchester when I was very young. You can find pictures of it easily enough: old stone and brick buildings, stones in the street, kids playing with sticks and balls. But I don't remember much about the city before the war.

I was five when the war began, and six when the bombing began in Manchester – by the time I was old enough to remember home, I'd left.

I do remember a few things. On one occasion when I was quite young, I fell and got a nail stuck in my hand, between the thumb and forefinger. My father was a small man, 145 pounds in his boxing days, but he carried me on his back all the way to the infirmary – I remember him saying I could have had lockjaw. I used to *love* going to the infirmary; the beds smelled beautiful. All my life I've loved that smell.

The infirmary wasn't exactly paradise, mind you. There was an orange rubber piece below the sheet, in case you pissed the bed; all they had for entertainment was a urinal. And of course you only ended up in the hospital in the first place if there was something wrong with you. But I looked forward to it, in an odd way. It was like going *inside* from the war and everything else, if that makes sense.

We went back to Stonyhurst once, years after the Blitz – Amy, Margaret, myself, and another young lady. Amy, the oldest, who was a mother to me at that time, said she'd rest by a ditch. But when she sat down the ground wasn't ground at all, but a hole. She folded right in half like sealing an envelope, legs up over her head. But the *expression* on her face – she was terrified, and her bum was in the water – the three of us couldn't help her, and couldn't help laughing either. Hysteria. One of the funniest things I've seen in my life. Is that a story worth telling? I couldn't tell you. Still, I like to remember it, to *visit* the story in my mind. And I like telling it. It brings other stories along with it..

You can have good memories of unhappy times, you know – it can feel good to remember difficult or unpleasant memories, and to get that part of yourself back for a moment.

There was a chap who lived nearby called Jimmy Grimley. Jimmy was a dancer in his heyday, in vaudeville. He was courting a lady named Gladys. They were quite old, I'd say in their late 50s—

Now, where we lived, the houses were clustered tightly together on the street: thirty-four on one side, and thirty-four on the other, with a step leading up to each house. One house at the end of a nearby street had a Pakistani or Indian fellow living there, and he had other people living in the *rafters* of his house. But not only his: that's how they lived all the way down the street. In those days Indians weren't buying restaurants, you know – they came over to live as best they could, but they were very poor, even poorer than the rest of us.

You had no hot running water. There was a coal fire; to have an occasional bath, you'd put a tin tub in front of the fire, with cold water, then a couple of pans of boiling hot water to make it lukewarm. Very primitive living – hard living.

At any rate, Jimmy Grimley would take Gladys out. Perhaps his own wife had died, and her husband – they'd go out, and he and Gladys were very much in love. Well, when they went to the pub on the corner, they had to pass our house on the way home. And Jimmy used to sing: 'When I grow too old to dream / I'll have you to remember...'

(My mum sang that song the morning she died.)

Jimmy would dance as they came down the street, sometimes quite late at night, after ten o'clock. People would yell down from the top window, —*Oh, stop singing!* (If they could open the window, of course.)

One particular woman, she went a bit further. In front of every house, on the sidewalk, was a grid, a grate, where you'd drop the coal down. And this woman, who lived further down the road from us, she was tired of Jimmy singing and dancing, one thing and the other. So one particular night, Jimmy was on his own, going out to see his lady friend further down. The woman down the road, she'd removed the grate from the hole in front of the house.

And down the hole he went.

Then the woman phoned the police, saying Jimmy was breaking and entering. And he'd broken his leg!

Well, that's the way things were. I wouldn't want you thinking there's no *drama* in this book.

When it comes to childhood, I'm short on dates. 1940, 1939? I can't remember exactly when we were evacuated. That was a long time ago, and knowing the date wouldn't change what it means to me.

But I know that we'd moved several times by then, as our houses had been bombed. We started off on Brindle St in Hulme, where I was born. Then we lived in Durham St, I believe, Bridge St, and Chatham St. After that we lived in Bark St – that one I remember well from after the war. When you move that many times in a short time, you can't bring things along every time. You leave behind so much, but you're still alive. Your life is the things you keep with you.

I couldn't tell you anymore which address was which year or month.

It was so long ago. In my memory I don't see the calendar, I see the way we lived, the way it felt: *These were the meals at Bridge Street. These are the games we played on Chatham Street.* That's how you tell time when it's passed.

All the men left in the city seemed to be wearing helmets. Most of the other men had already gone into the forces. In America they go on about 'supporting the troops,' but in those days, there were troops and troops, so to speak. As children, we looked on the Air Force men as a little more intelligent than the Army or Navy. And if you went into the Navy, in those baggy trousers, most people felt you weren't involved in the war, as you were on a bleeding ship three miles from anywhere, just firing guns.

Well – we were children. We didn't understand about things like Dunkirk, or U-boats, or merchant ships being sunk at sea. We just looked at the Army men, for instance, and figured the smart ones were officers. A lot of people volunteered for the Army – men who weren't married, or who wanted to get away from their wives or families for whatever reason. They'd give you a uniform, a warm bed, an overcoat. A lot of people were better off in the Army. It was an escape from normal life at home, waiting for bombs to fall.

Dad had volunteered for the Army when he was 16, and was sent to Ireland. That was 1916. He told us that the biggest danger there was goats running wild; they had more trouble fighting each other than with the Irish, he said. He was lucky too.

Anyhow, if someone volunteered for the Army, and his wife was seen with another man while her husband away, walking or in the pub, the man would be sorted out by others in the neighbourhood. The men who were left in the city, people would remark to them, —Why aren't you in the Army? You'd wonder, *Was it his eyes, or his back? Or was he a coward?*

Decent people will say unkind things, and not only in wartime.

The lady across the road had a young baby girl, two years of age. One day the baby ran down across the street and into our home. Dad walked out across the street to the lady's house, bringing the little girl with him. And the lady berated her: — Don't you ever *ever* go in there again! She was quite right, but Dad took it to heart. He took it badly. The woman meant, *Don't do that anywhere;* but Dad thought she just meant him: *Don't ever go near Mr Holland.* The lady even explained that to him, but it had a big effect on my Dad for quite a while. A day and a half. He was so upset.

One of those little things I've always remembered.

Here's another, since it's just us talking:

We used to build bonfires in one of the larger streets above where we lived. It's amazing, when you talk about bonfires, how much you could get from an 'empty' house. When people moved on they'd just leave certain things behind, if they couldn't lift them. Bits of furniture and so on. It needed to be chopped up, so there was firewood to use in a fire of a night. Then you'd make cocoa, and roast potatoes and nuts in the fire. There wasn't much schooling to be done (which I didn't mind). I suppose that's just how life was.

I was home in late 1943. There wasn't as much danger by that time. The city was in ruins, so we'd gather up the pieces and drink cocoa around the fire.

I couldn't give you a proper date for the Blitz, you know. But I remember all the barrage balloons in the air, made at Dunlop's where Dad worked, a mile or two from where I lived. Bombs and rockets would come down, like the V-2, making that sound...when the sound *stopped*, you knew it had come.

When you'd hear an air raid warning, you'd go with your family to an air raid shelter. Now, we had two large double beds

– for Mum and Dad, and for myself and my sister. And during the air raid, we'd hear the siren and take one mattress with us to the school, half a mile away, or else to a large building in the area. We'd hide in the cellar, and put the mattress down. There was a lot of space. And rats, of course.

The air raid siren would go off, and you'd walk together to safety. A bomb might have fallen on the street the night before, 24 hours ago, and the building next to you would still be smoldering. And there's the air raid warden in his helmet, making sure you went to the right place. In the shelter, you hoped to be sleeping next to somebody you knew, but that wasn't always the case. People would come in who'd been drinking, quite drunk. The men would walk forward to them, carry them out, give them a few punches, and tell them to piss off. You didn't want them running around with the children.

Just because we pulled together doesn't mean you could trust *everyone*, of course.

Behind our house was a small yard, a few yards deep, then a narrow alleyway, then the next house. On a few occasions you'd get people trying to break into your house to rob you. It was quite easy to climb over the wall. My father told me about the time two men came around trying to rob a house, and the chap who lived there was a professional wrestler. He let them get *into* the yard alright. And then he went out to them, picked them up, and threw them both over the back wall. But one of them ended up crippled – and the wrestler was put away in prison, for using excessive force. I suppose the thieves had already been punished enough.

You had lots of pickpockets as well. Later in the war, when you'd take a day out and go to Blackpool with sandwiches and a bottle of lemonade, you'd have pickpockets on the trains. Or someone on the train would offer a game of cards, and pull somebody else in, a *drifter*, to lose a game or two on purpose. He was part of the fix. Then on the bigger stake he might ask for one card and get three new ones, *by accident* of course, and take the tourists' money.

At my age you think back on these things and realize how much the world has changed; and you wonder *when* it changed, exactly.

You did have a lot of thieves in those days. On the other hand, you couldn't get anything without a ration book. That didn't make it right, but some people felt they had no choice. The doctor was free, of course, but he'd give you the same bottle of medicine for headache, the flu, or cancer. It was terrible – the odor alone!

And it's not as if you were having a bath every week. A bath was a *goldmine*. We'd get a bath at the school. Dad would go swimming, just to get a chance to use the showers, at the baths – miles away from the house. He'd ride the bus there after work, or his bike. That's how Dad kept clean.

The bombing was a big part of our lives then, but even though it *touched* everything, it wasn't everything. Mostly you tried to get on with your life, if you could. Some people couldn't. As I say, I was lucky. If you pick up a history of that time in England, you read about the Blitz, the war, the 'home front.' But that's a story about a nation, and I was only a boy.

We found ways to live, since we had no choice.

We'd have a 'party': we'd eat sardine sandwiches, which were the *big thing*; marmalade and jam or a blancmange, and a mustard pickle, but sweet and sugary. You could have either bread and jam, or buttered toast – but not jam *and* butter together, because you had to make them last, stretch them out.

The bread was better then, than what I buy now. Better tasting.

Though perhaps I just remember it that way.

We'd eat margarine instead of butter, which cost extra stamps. And chocolate was a special treat – extra coupons. Of a weekend, you'd go to the movies. I was a movie buff at that age – still am. We'd go with our cousins: Amy and Teddy were the two oldest, then Margaret and my sister, and myself. They'd carry me and swing me by my arms, depending on who had the money, or Teddy would carry me on his shoulders. I remember one of the movies we saw, the star was Ida Lupino. She had a famous uncle named Lupino Lane who was around at the same time as Stanley Holloway. I saw him in vaudeville in 1939, at the Hippodrome, with Dad.

Anyhow, the weekend we went to the pictures and saw Ida Lupino, she came onscreen, and she had a club foot. But I didn't know that. So when I saw her, I called out, —*Why is she wearing odd shoes?*

Everyone in the cinema laughed at me. I didn't know what I was saying.

When you're ad libbing, sometimes that's how it is. (There's a bit of 'insider' comedy advice for you.)

Teachers at school would condemn me sometimes, when I made a remark. —*Holland, none of that!* But as a boy, I had a sense of humour. Half the time I didn't understand the words I was saying, it was just lines I'd heard in a movie. But if it got a laugh, I'd repeat it. It's how you learn. And that's how I've stayed, as I've gotten older. You don't need any education to get a laugh, thank God.

The day my mum died, at 8:30 in the morning, she sang two songs: '*When I grow too old to dream...I'll have you to remember,*' and '*I'm in love with two sweethearts, and they're both in love with me...*' It's hard for me to hear those songs now. No matter where

I am, I hear them, and suddenly I'm *there*, and it's my mum singing. And she's singing about us.

Dad would send her good money when he worked away. We weren't wealthy, but Mum had a bit to spend. And she was a silly woman, in a way. She'd buy drinks for everybody and have people over, and share some of the meat, tomatoes, and onions. She used to get good money off my dad, and that was her way – and she was like a wild dancer at times, climbing on top of the table and singing. My sister was exactly the same – she sang with a band, and became a model. She was a very beautiful. They both were.

I don't want to dwell on my sister. She was a model, she sang, she made a bit of money. She was like Ava Gardner. She passed away a few months before Cata – I didn't know that until later. I wish her well, wherever she is now. And I don't want to say more.

My mother was very well loved. She'd helped a lot of people. We'd have people over to the house of a weekend, and she'd make sure every one of them had a good meal. And *then* she'd remember she had two children of her own to feed...

Dad would come home of a weekend, he'd join in, and the house would be full of life, like Mum was. We never thought of buying anymore bleeding *furniture* to replace what was bombed out, of course...

Our home in Bridge St was was bombed out one night while we were away, so that was no use. Across Chatham street from us, later, was a family called the Muirheads: a famous name, though they weren't a famous family. But I'll always remember them. My sister and I used to cross Chatham St to have a bath over there – two boys in one tin, two girls in another. The entire Muirhead family was killed when a bomb fell on them. Just like that.

My mum had tuberculosis, I believe. I remember her coughing terribly. When I got back to Manchester after the evacuation, she was quite frail. She died when I was young, but I have good memories of her, happy memories, to go with the memories of her passing.

Mum wasn't *eccentric*, exactly. Just lively, alive. I always remember when she would bathe me as a baby, she'd stand me on the table, and when she washed my private parts, she'd say,

—And how's your little pigeon today?

An innocent thing. You know, that might be my earliest memory, so properly speaking it should have gone on the very first page. But you can't start your first book off talking about your little pigeon, can you. Where would you go from there?

I think my mother was 43 when she died, during the war. I believe it was 1944. We were home on a Saturday morning. Was it September? I think so. We'd put her in a bed in the parlour, downstairs. People were coming to see her, to pay their respects. She knew she was dying, of course. I suppose we all knew.

In the morning, my father came into the living room and said,

—She's gone, son. And no one will ever take her place.

I ran out of the house and across one of the busiest streets in the city – *lucky* – and kept running for a whole mile, to my uncle Freddie's house, where Amy and Teddy and Margaret lived.

I went to live with them later, when they moved into a more civilized house provided by the government.

I believe I was ten when Mum died. It's funny, the things you remember clearly and the things you don't. You'd think the exact date would be so important, but some days I can't even remember the *year*. But I remember running. I was *fast*, as well.

Mum would go to a pub called the Nudger, on Stretford Road near where we lived. A woman named Nelly Kelly ran the place. We'd lived on Durham Street before that, but I couldn't tell you when we moved.

When I think of Mum I remember Nelly Kelly and Durham Street, and the whole city is *there*. It's all inside me, and it only needs telling. But memories aren't exactly stories; they're all out of order—

When I played for Stamford Albion, years later, two of the main players lived on Durham St – I can't remember their names, but they were the instigation for me joining the team. I had quite a name early on, as a little player. Albert Scanlon, my pal who played for United, played for Stamford Albion then as well. Further down the road was another pub called Clynes's. A fellow named Dennis Jones played for their team in the same position as Albert, and at the time I'd say he was the better player.

We were on Brindle St before that, where I was born. We lived in the house behind Clynes's. Everyone knew the name because of their soccer team. The Fletchers owned the pub, and they wanted to adopt my sister – she was a beautiful child. Their backyard was next to ours, and they'd throw sweets over the wall to us. Further down Brindle St was Mr Hulme, the same name as the district where we lived later on, on Bark St. I remember him, though I was only a baby of three or four, because he was always covered in black dust. He used to deliver coal wearing a big carrier on his back. Like the men in *Spartacus*, with iron strips across. Well, not *exactly* like that, I suppose.

All I can remember of Mr Hulme is his eyes; the rest of him was pitch black.

On the corner by Cambridge St was a shop called Joe Purcelli's, I believe. I went to school with his son – a good soccer player with black curly hair like me. After the war, Purcelli's shop did marvelous business and became very well-known. It's a good job they made it through the war in the first place: during the bombing, a mine landed directly in front of his shop, but didn't explode. It was like an egg, burgundy colour, four feet high – like a chocolate you'd have at Easter. They turned it up and collected money inside. Not that they could collect too much: they had to empty it daily, otherwise people would steal it. People didn't even have the money to put *in*, really. Eventually the army sent people round to detonate it.

I couldn't tell you the date that happened, now. By carrying the memory with me, I carry part of the city around. I don't even need to hold onto it. It's part of who I am.

Facing Clynes's was the Mitre, owned by William Meredith; in his time he was the greatest soccer player in all of Britain. He played for Manchester City, and then joined United. They gave him a public house to run when he retired, but he never drank. I was introduced to him once – it was a big thing to me. My dad was his pal. Dad had trials for Aston Villa, you know; he said he wasn't good enough, but I think it's that he wasn't getting enough food. Those were rough years. In those days, if an Irishman had a good pair of shoes he was doing well.

Anyhow, Dad married young instead, and found other things to do in his life.

Dad said to me, —And no one will ever take her place.

I ran out the door and down the street, five streets down from Stretford Rd, one of the busiest streets in Manchester. I ran blindly across, I didn't even look. Ten years of age. God was with me that I wasn't hit by a car or bus; I suppose He wanted to read the rest of this book. And so I made it safely to Unkie's.

Unkie was Dad's brother. He had three children, my cousins Amy, Margaret, and Teddy, and walked with a bent knee. I moved in with them when I was twelve years old, after Mum had died and Dad was away working. My sister would stay at a friend's house, and I'd go down to Unkie's.

I'd become a thief, you see. I'll talk about that later.

(I'd also taken up smoking. One night I lit a cigarette in bed and set the pillow on fire. Unkie threw me out and told me to go home. But I didn't quit smoking until my eldest son was born, thirty years later.)

After I'd moved back in with Dad, I'd still go down during the day to see Unkie and my cousins. My other uncle Albert, who I didn't know very well, was a mathematician. Brilliant. He worked for William Hill, one of the biggest bookmakers in Britain. My father and Albert, the youngest and an alcoholic, they worked for William Hill the day he won £33,000 in Yorkshire.

Not to say it was only *good* luck with Uncle Albert. I went down there one day, and picked up his Dowd's Lemonade bottle and drank it. But it wasn't lemonade at all, for some reason it was full of methylated spirits. Off to the hospital again. I'd been to Blackburn Infirmary during the war – I was six, I think, and had my tonsils out. I remember that I wasn't supposed to drink during recovery, but I got up in the middle of a night and had some water. It was as if somebody'd put a knife in my throat – three extra days in hospital for one glass of water!

The infirmary became famous, or 'infamous' I suppose, years later when a baby was stolen from its parents there. You can't blame me for that – I was nowhere near it at the time.

I never realized how close France was to England until I joined the airline as a steward and flew over the channel. When

I was a boy we were frightened of the war, it was *coming*. But it was also far away. The war was across the water and all around us.

At the back of our street was St Augustine's Church, and a big air raid shelter. At the corner of the street was a secondhand shop with three steps leading up to it and a fan-light in the roof. The owner was a German woman – she was opening it at night, and flashing signals to the Luftwaffe above. She was arrested for it, of course. Across the street was Paulden's. Lord Haw-Haw would come on the radio and say, —*Oh, we're very sorry about hitting Paulding's last night. We were trying to hit Dunlop's, you know! But we'll come back and see you. By the way, make sure you get into the air raid shelter...*

The army captured Lord Haw-Haw in Germany at the end of the war. His real name was William Joyce. And they hanged him.

We had battery-powered radios, and there were other people we liked to listen to instead. Some shows you didn't want to miss – like *Ramsbottom, Enoch, and Me.* You'd have the *Happidrome*, Tommy Handley. There was Sandy Powell: 'Can you hear me, mother?' Arthur Askey, a small man with glasses. George Formby, who looked very much like my father, with his hair parted down the center. (Dad's hair would get wavy if he didn't put water on it.) Formby would sing: 'I'm leaning on a lamp-post at the corner of the street, in case a certain little lady comes by...Oh me, oh my, I hope the little lady comes by...' That sort of thing was big in those days.

I was three years old when that song first came on the radio. I didn't know I remembered it until I remembered it, if that makes sense.

I cry with happiness, thinking of songs like those. It's embarrassing, as I get older, but I don't mind so much. I'll be out at Dina's in the village for a glass of wine, talking to someone and remembering, and I'll cry. But it's not just recalling a fact or image – it's like falling into a whirlpool. You can't stay in one spot, you get pulled around and around. It's amazing, even today in my apartment – I'll remember a smell, the fern and bracken, the nuts and primrose and snowdrops, the river in Hurst Green...

I'll always remember my father coming to Stonyhurst to visit. He was in the fire service in those days. He brought a bar of chocolate with *152 pieces* – it was like the side of a table, direct from the factory where he'd been working or something. I'd never seen chocolate so big. He'd left his job at Dunlop's, I can't remember exactly why. He had two overcoats, one grey one brown – raglan – and two suits, one with navy blue stripes, one brown and white stripes. To look presentable. But during the war, at certain times, those overcoats would go into the pawn shop. I think he'd get half a crown for them.

You have to look presentable, but your family has to eat, as well.

I talk about how hard it was, and it *was* hard, you know. But a lot of young people were less fortunate than me during the war – they weren't sent off to paradise like I was.

CHAPTER 2

Evacuation, homecoming

We can't just go in order, year by year – that's not how my memories fit together, and this isn't history, it's a story. So when I tell you about the evacuation, where I was during the second world war, it may make sense for me to jump ahead and talk about Korea, all the way on the other side of the world.

Forgive me.

In 1940 I was evacuated to Hurst Green, Lancashire, near Clitheroe. I think of us as going to to 'Stonyhurst' as much as Hurst Green, because Stonyhurst College is there. It's very famous – the largest Jesuit college in Britain. George HW Bush's grandfather went there, and Mr Tolkien wrote some of his hobbit stories there. He based parts of them on the countryside around Stonyhurst. That's ancient history now, but *The Hobbit* was still a new book when I arrived at Stonyhurst. And even ancient things are still alive, in the English countryside.

As for me, I only ever *visited* the school itself, which is why they don't mention me on their tours. Stonyhurst changed during the war as well: when I arrived it was all priests in smocks, then the next week they all had uniforms on. It was as if they'd all become officers.

Two thirds of the children in Manchester were evacuated during the war; families in the country took us in. Some of us didn't see our parents for months or even years. It sounds terrible, and of course it was; I missed my parents so much. But I was happy, in a way.

I don't know how many of us traveled together, nor the date we went. It's like when my youngest son asked where my own dad went to school – I never knew he *went* to school. He must have, but I never thought to ask him.

The coach to Clitheroe wasn't just our crowd; it was children bound for different parts of the village, to stay with different families. My cousins Amy (the eldest), Teddy, and Margaret went with me to Hurst Green. My sister went also, who was Margaret's age.

Like a lot of groups of kids, when we arrived, we were split up: Amy in one house, Teddy and me in another, Margaret and my sister in a third. At first I was put with an old gamekeeper, whom we called 'Grandfather,' and his daughter, who was what they call a 'spinster.' Not wanting to say anything unkind, I have to admit she wasn't a very nice person. She was determined that we would not get all that we wanted. They were paid to take us in, but it didn't pass down to us at all in return.

One of our neighbours used to have a patch of potatoes that needed picking – he paid Teddy and me sixpence to extricate them. It was great to make the money...but the woman we lived with would take the money off us. Can you imagine? We were six years old, and she was stealing our wages!

Breakfast was one sausage and half a tomato, or one sausage and one egg – beautifully cooked, but still... We ate a lot of rabbit as well, as Grandfather didn't have to go far to get them.

I was moved from their home later on. Not everyone would accept evacuees, or could, and sometimes you had a bad match. That was understandable – it created a completely different way of life for the couples that took in children, and that could be hard. I was taken in by 'Grandma,' who lived in Delph Cottages, #8 Quality Row, if I remember right. (Why would I tell you the address? Why would I remember? But I do.) There were five cottages, with outside toilets, very close together. Kathleen and Dickie Rogerson were next door, living with 'Grandad.' He was a wonderful old gentleman, like my 'Grandma' Osbaldeston.

Outside the door of each cottage you had flowers growing: primrose, tulips, snowdrops, and a purple flower whose name I never knew. Cobblestone walkways connected the five cottages, each with a wooden gate and steps leading down to a sunken garden. Behind the cottages a stream flowed, and Dickie and I would go and catch trout by hand. They'd hide under the stones, and we could put our hands underneath – slowly, careful not to splash! – and grab them under the belly. Or you could take a tree branch with cotton and sort of fish them out.

Like so many things, it was primitive, but it worked well enough.

The cottages were called 'two up, two down' – a kitchen and sitting room downstairs, two bedrooms upstairs. I lived in the bedroom at the back of the house, and could jump out of the top window onto a hill at the back, with a dilapidated hen-hut. It was our hideout: Dickie and me would go in there to play Cowboys & Indians. (Which is funny in a way, because England never had cowboys, or that sort of 'Indians.' But we did have Western movies.)

Down by the stream, a road curved down to the left, and a gentleman named Isaacs lived there. He owned the property down there, and part of the road. You'd go out behind Mr Isaacs's house onto a road that led to the village, which was a few hundred yards away.

It was about 500 yards up to the main lodge, belonging to the owner of the cottages. He was the owner of the Franklin House.

As you'd follow the stream to the Franklin House, you'd come to a wooden bridge. Below that, it was fenced off, and the trout would gather there.

If you followed the road up to the village, you'd come to the Shamrock Woods; in the woods was Bottle Cottage. It was absolutely beautiful, deep green, with animal sounds everywhere, and a fresh smell – Dickie and I would look for owls' nests there. In the summer we'd put on shorts and soak in the water. It seemed so deep...

The last time I traveled to Hurst Green was about ten years ago, with Bob Burrows. We went back there, to the stream and the pool. It had seemed so grand when I was small. But do you know, the water's only about a foot deep! It's the same as the church: I thought it was gigantic as a child, but it's just a small country church. To a child's mind, I suppose everything seems grand that way. The stream, the woods, the war.

The people on the block were good neighbours, and I'm not just saying that. When we'd go out to pick blackberries or elderberries, it was always as a block, a group. Of course, not *everyone* was equally friendly. Isaacs would not allow traffic to go down to his road to deliver coal for the fire. No sir! He'd make them stop at the gate outside his house...which meant that they would have to walk along the road, carrying the coal on their backs, or go to the back of the house and come down the hill, without falling over if they could manage it. When the coal was delivered, everybody would go out and jeer at Isaacs. The madding crowd!

If you didn't have a walking stick or a branch you could wave your fists, I suppose. I can't remember seeing the man, honestly. But Isaacs was the baddie, keeping us from getting our coal. I think it was nice to be a bit angry at the man down the road, instead of the Germans.

Now that I think of it, the Franklin House would never allow Dickie and me to get near the fish, where they were breeding. There was a rivalry of sorts in the village, I suppose. There always are in those little places.

But we were together all the same, because we had to be. We'd all go out and pick bracken from the Shamrock Woods, where the wild owl was. They were *his* woods. Dickie and I would go looking for it, and when we saw it, it was *terrifying*. We were fine thinking about the owl, looking for it, but finding it... You might say we had the wrong kind of bravery, that looking was fine but finding was too much for us.

Well, we were children.

Everyone who was around the cottages during the day would go into the forest together to collect bracken – twigs to burn – and blackberries and windberries. The ladies in the houses used to bake bread and share it with each other, and with us. Rationing was on, of course, but this was something else, something private. They'd put white butter on the bread, and I've never tasted bread as good in my entire life. Grandma had relations who would visit on weekends, but just for the day, as there was no place for them to sleep. There was Uncle Tom, and Uncle Jack who had a shop in Blackburn. Uncle Jack's two children were Sheila, who became a nurse, and Jackie. Jackie was a student; he had blond hair parted at the side. A good-looking boy of fourteen. He'd wear a green cap with yellow braiding, his school cap. I idolized him, and the thing I most wanted in my life, then, was his cap.

Kathleen was in love with Jackie, which was understandable. His hair was in a quiff, and his cap wouldn't come over the front;

it would sit on the back of his head, somewhat...is the word 'nonchalant'? No, *flamboyant* – well, he was a handsome swine.

And I was in love with Sheila. Well – 'in love,' at six years old. I think she was twenty years old, and to me, the prettiest person in the world.

Jack's wife and Tom's wife were quite nice to us. Uncle Tom hit me once: he was sat on the chair, and I went up behind him and ruffled his hair. Just playing around. But it was stuck on the back of his head – it was a toupee! And he did give me a whack, which frightened me less than the toupee itself. I had no idea what one was.

That was the only time, though.

Grandma had three sons: a dance-band leader, a teacher, and (if memory serves) a priest. Now, the house was very small, so while you might get everybody in, they wouldn't be able to sit down. But it was so important for them all to be there. Can you imagine? There was no choice, really – you had to have them in, and you'd make do.

The family would always bring me something: food and sweets, usually, because they had shops in the city. Even with the rationing, we got the cream of it. I suppose Grandma had a little more money than Grandad, next door. We'd go to the shops nearby for clothes, and she certainly dressed me better than he did. Whatever I got, I shared with Dickie and Kathleen – of course I did, we loved each other. They were my family, during that time.

If Grandma's family didn't come down on a Sunday and run us to church, we'd walk with Dickie and Kathleen, perhaps two or three miles. I believe the church was on the grounds of Stonyhurst College. It's hard to remember, of course, as I was only young. (I suppose I got older.)

For a grand day out we'd go to Clitheroe and buy meat pies, which were popular during the war, I think because you don't need *good* meat for them. You could buy them in pubs, and boiled eggs in vinegar. Working people would call in on the way home; that might be their one meal for the *day*, a meat pie or an egg. Can you imagine? And those were the working people, the ones who could count on a wage.

One of the most wonderful things in my life was, at Christmas, to get some cardboard, and cut it in a rectangle. We'd go to the wallpaper shop in Clitheroe, and ask them for the old sample books. We'd take pages from the sample books and stick them onto the cardboard, and then paste a beautiful picture – perhaps a painting of Our Lord – and a calendar with it. Those were our Advent calendars, and that was our special treat at Christmas. It was only simple.

Last Christmas, meanwhile, my son ordered me a book about Manchester. I gather he bought it on the Internet with a credit card, directly from the author in England, all while sitting at his desk. Two days later it turned up on my doorstep. It's a wonderful book, don't get me wrong, but it's only *history*. I'll never think on it and cry, as I do with those little squares of wallpaper. As I'm doing even now.

You'll notice I haven't mentioned going to school in Hurst Green. There's a simple reason: I didn't particularly go.

I have one memory of school in Hurst Green, the day my cousin won a raffle. They gave her a shoebox full of paper – bloody typical – but when she pulled everything out, she found a one-shilling piece wrapped up inside. There are twenty shillings to a pound, so it may not sound like a lot of money, but to a child in 1941 or so...

I can't remember the name of the children's school at Hurst Green because I never spent much time there. I was in an accident, you see.

Two boys were throwing slate roof shingles to each other. I don't know how they came by them; during the war you'd have materials scattered about. One of the boys was named Vincent Pryor; the other was named Scofield. Oddly enough, when we lived in Bark Street in Manchester, Scofield's family lived across the alley in the back of our house. A few yards further down from where *he* lived was a pub, and next door was Arthur Boswell's house. I had a fight with Boswell once; we were both small (he ended up a professional jockey, actually), but all the same, when he hit me on the nose, I thought *Oh that's it, you've won.* Maybe he's the reason I've got a blob nose.

That was a different sort of 'seeing stars' from the type that comes later in this book.

I wish I remembered more about Boswell. I'm sure he didn't go around hitting people *all* the time.

Anyhow, as you walk down the long path to Stonyhurst College, there are two concrete pillars. You pass through them into the countryside. To the left is Bailey's house, where 'Squire Bailey' lives, or lived. The Baileys go back centuries in that area – they're the top family, so to speak. My sister and Margaret lived there, but they used to put pinafores and uniforms on the two of them and use them as *maids*, cleaning and washing, even though they were just young girls, nine years old.

Beyond the two pillars you head toward the area where Teddy and I were first billeted, and come to the Fells: the hunting grounds full of rabbits and birds, where Grandpa would take me while he worked as a gamekeeper.

Well, Pryor and Scofield were throwing slates to each other across the road, near the pillars. I was outside the Baileys' house.

Do you know the expression, 'I never knew what hit me?' I *knew*, I just couldn't do anything about it.

I was leaning against this pillar, and the slates were coming from each side. One came toward me, and I put my arms up to stop it, and it went right between my hands. It was only a little thing.

But it damaged the nerves in my eyes. Due to that injury, and the limited medical attention that was available, I never went to school after that. My eye had to be bathed every day. I used to get *matter* seeping from my eyes. I didn't know more about it than that. I was six or seven years old, I'd only been in Hurst Green a short time, and I didn't go to school again until I was back in Manchester.

I was living with my cousin then, in Grandfather's house. And my family were nearby: Amy lived a hundred yards away, my sister and Margaret were in the Bailey home, and Grandfather was kind to all of us.

Amy was the eldest of the family. She would have been about fifteen then, becoming a young woman, so to speak. The people she lived with were very nice. Everybody loved cousin Amy. She later became my caretaker-mother, when I went to live with her, Teddy, and Margaret after my mum died.

Teddy was allowed to go back home to his father first; I'm not sure why. I think certain children could return home before the evacuation concluded, with special permission. But me being a small boy, I wasn't allowed. Nor did I wish to go – I was happier where I was than in Manchester, where the bombs were! I loved *every moment*, every inch of the earth, in Hurst Green.

One way I can travel, now that I'm a bit older, is by remembering.

I remember walking from the Stonyhurst mile to the Bailey mansion, down that way, and to Over Hacking, a wood near the school. I remember the two rivers, the Ribble and the Hodder, and going swimming in the water as a boy with so many fish swimming nearby, all around me. And I remember the day Peter King, the boy with a Barbadian father, went into the water to save me from drowning.

(I was only ever 4'10" even at age 15, and a terrible swimmer, so you can imagine I was glad of his help.)

You know, for someone who can hardly swim, I've got a lot of happy memories of those rivers. As you get toward Clitheroe, there's a bridge that crosses the water, the Cromwell Bridge. There's no rails to it, just a walkway a few feet wide, covered in moss and old stones. If I remember rightly it's got three arches underneath. The legend – which I was inclined to believe, since it frightened me – was that it would draw you down to the water if you tried to look down. Magnetic!

A few miles away from Hurst Green is Oliver Cromwell's courtroom. But since I've left, I'm told he's seldom there.

The accident affected the nerves in my eye, and caused me real trouble – I've always needed glasses, and perhaps that piece of slate has something to do with it. On the other hand, it saved me having to go to school. I don't know whether it was worth it. But that's life, isn't it? You don't always know.

At any rate, I had no real education until I was nine or ten years of age. When I returned to Manchester I started going to school again, but while we were in Hurst Green I ran wild. And I still do, though I don't run as quickly anymore.

That damned slate even affected my time in the Army. I went to Korea on the *Empire Pride*; during the voyage we'd head to the back of the ship, and they'd put coloured balloons in the water. We'd be given guns – to keep us busy, I suppose – and we had to hit so many balloons to qualify. The sergeant came back after I'd done my test and said, —You've not hit *one* balloon.

—It's my eyes, isn't it.

—It must be.

—Then can I go back into my cabin and read my book?

No response to that.

The news was either good or bad, depending your point of view: —You will not be allowed to join any regiment, Holland, because your eyes are bad.

Wisely I said, —Well, the chap who did my eyes told me that, you're not telling me anything new.

He nearly put me on a charge! It's too late for me to get in trouble for it now, which is why I'm telling *you*.

To this day I don't know if Scofield and Pryor ever knew what happened to my eye. I wonder about that. Or to use a word I rather enjoy, for some reason: I *ponder*. Not to be confused with 'powder,' from my skin care days.

Kathleen Rogerson married an older man and had seven children. Dickie had two sons, both good soccer players. I kept in touch with them for years, and with Grandma, to whom I'd write letters and sometimes visit. I can't remember when she passed away, but I remember being in Egypt, on the way to Korea, and getting a letter onboard ship. *'This is the last time I'll write to you,'* it said, *'as I am losing my sight.'*

Dickie was my pal, and Kathleen his sister I loved. They were my world.

In the end, in 1944, I was the last one to go home to Manchester along with two girls named Margaret Pearson and

Monica Killey – but after a couple of days I went *back* to Hurst Green for a couple of weeks. I've often wondered about that; I never knew why. I know I was the last evacuee to leave Hurst Green, and—

Well.

You know, I probably didn't leave the village at all, that first time. I remember Margaret and Monica, but it makes no sense that I'd go and come back – I must have just stayed an extra two weeks, and misremembered.

My sister had come home well before me, as she was three years older, and could take better care of herself in the city. I should imagine that's how they decided – how much danger the children were in. I hope so. *We* certainly didn't want to come home. We had the best of everything in the countryside, or that's how it felt. It was...a dreamworld.

I was the youngest of our crowd, and always imagined that was why they kept me in the country after everyone else. I didn't understand the other reason, I suppose the *real* reason, until much later: my mum was dying.

CHAPTER 3

Dreamworld

The results of the Hillsborough inquest came through this year. I wasn't aware of the disaster when it occurred, as it didn't receive the same attention in the United States, though I heard about it in time. A terrible thing. It was bound to happen eventually; and of course, it wasn't the first time.

In 1946, Stoke City had a terrible disaster. I think there were 33 killed. I was a child then, but we all knew about it. That was the worst until the disaster at Sheffield. I was away, then.

Of course, the government *is* at fault. They didn't have the apparatus or organization to look after the people there if anything went wrong.

Americans talk about football – their football – as a religion. I know just what they mean, but I'm not sure they understand what football is in Europe and South America. It touches every part of your life.

The team that I played for briefly, Stamford Albion – with my pal Albert Scanlon, who went on to play for United – while I was away working, seven of the lads had gone to watch City playing Huddersfield, a Cup tie in Bolton, I think. And five of them were killed in a car accident. I never knew the details, nor did I wish to; it was too much. Too terrible.

Albert had experienced that as well, and to survive it... I remember hearing that they had to feed him through his *feet*, through a tube, after the crash.

But Albert survived Munich. He played in every game the next season.

When someone from Manchester says 'Munich,' you know what he means without him saying. That's what I mean when I say it touches your whole life. If I talk about the Germans, the war, that's one thing. That was my life as a very young boy. But if I'm talking with someone from those days and one of us mentions 'Munich,' it's something we share. Some of us knew people on the plane, the 'Busby Babes,' but *everyone* thought of them. They were our *dream*.

Nowadays, football stadiums can go five or ten times as high up as they used to. You can go for the game and have several experiences all at once. It's nothing like it used to be. Well: the same with hospitals, or food, or television, I suppose. We had no way of knowing what we *didn't* have.

When I think about being poor, I often joke about Oliver Twist. You had canals running across city, and dead dogs or cats being thrown in there, and the RSPCA would come fish them out... In Smithfield Market, the center of Manchester at that time, they'd sell fish, and in the early hours of the morning, the ground would be infested with rats; you'd see them running all around. My father's relative was a rat-catcher. He'd wear a top hat, like you see in a picture of Abraham Lincoln. He'd see a rat running and put the hat over it to catch it. It seems childish, in a way: *simple*.

We'd have 35 houses in a single block, with outside toilets. This kind of low life, poor life, was still prevalent in the late Forties. It stayed that way until well after war. There was a world of difference between haves and have-nots, and at times it seemed like *all* of us were have-nots... At least the people you could actually see. The ones with money, you could never get close to. And they certainly wouldn't get close to you.

During the war there was a sense of duty or commitment from the government – they gave us food stamps. And even the rich, they couldn't get food without the food stamps. (That's where the black market came in. It wouldn't take long to have a few extra books printed. You could get cigarettes, silk stockings, food, perfume, things like that.) But it cut both ways – during the war, if there was a fire in a house, it wasn't given a great deal of concern. A factory building munitions, where bombs might go off, or shelters – of course they'd deal with it right away. But with a house, they might just let it burn. The government had its priorities.

You cannot be romantic about the war; it was a war, and we had nothing. It wasn't as simple as 'fighting for England.' Those who volunteered to serve their country, half of them went because there was no bloody food! And they'd get a uniform to keep them warm. It was the same with me, years later – I didn't volunteer because I was brave, I was just fed up with the food in England. But in my mind I also thought: It'll give me a chance to see another country. I wanted to travel – if I was in a dreamworld, what was the *rest* of the world like?

(And I was, you know. The biggest thing in my life, bar my parents, was to read the *Champion*, Rusty Gale, the *Wizard*, the *Hotspur*, the *Rover*. As a kid I could be quite quick, but I didn't get it from school, it was due to Uncle Albert, Uncle Teddy, my Dad...)

Your father and mother might go out and have a drink, but they would have two halves of a single pint. And they *needed* a drink, as well. Luckily there was a pub on every other street.

Mum and Dad would say they were going out for a drink, and if perchance something happened or you ran out of firewood, you could run to the pub – and you *would* run, you wouldn't walk – and wait outside for them to come out. But you could also walk in, and everyone knew everyone, and would look out for you: —Aye aye Wally, you've got the lad here! And some people would give you a penny to buy a packet of chocolate powder, folded into a paper cone. You could dip your finger in and eat the powder off your finger.

A disgusting way of doing things, really. On the other hand, it was *chocolate powder...*

And it was a gift. No one could give much, but what they had, they gave.

From a child's point of view, the war might mean something as simple as, *you didn't have to go to school.* —OK lads, what are we going to do? And you'd play football, if you had a ball, that is. Sometimes you'd go to another part of town, and they'd have a 'casey': an old soccer ball that had been stitched up with string. It wouldn't be fully blown up either, so when it hit you it *popped* on your head. Half the time it would just drop to the ground.

And then you'd look around for shrapnel, and if any of the factories in the center of Manchester had been hit (and they were), you'd head down there and roam through the factories. They'd been left as they were. There weren't people to clean them out instantly. Many times you'd find things that you shouldn't take. It wasn't looked on as stealing, it was: Well, if you've not bothered to take it then *we'll* have it.

What you had, you gave, and what you needed, you took. That was another way the war touched everything.

I remember in 1949 getting a tour of a textile factory, for any of us interested in going into design as a trade. They had these photographs from the 30s of movie stars, with wavy hair, freshly combed, and colour photographs of people modeling different garments. Very old-fashioned. They let us have them, free, and we hung them up in the bedroom. It was something and it was available.

When I talk about those years – the war didn't end when it ended, if that makes sense. Everything was changed, and looking back, it was strange.

A lot of young people got grey hair. As a child you'd think: If they've got grey hair they're very old. But they weren't.

And you'd see old people and women without coats, wearing only a shawl. To see an old lady walking down the street, and most of them stooped, their heads bent...

Now that I'm older, I think about them. I see them differently, now.

If you could steal a loaf of bread – we'd be making our way back from the baths, on our own, and we'd go into the bottom of a store and steal a loaf. We could do it easily, and share it amongst the lads. Many times they'd throw a roll out after a few days, when it got moldy. And if they were a decent size, we'd grab them and throw them at the old people. I know it sounds cruel – but children do cruel things because they're ignorant.

If there was a guy wearing a hat and you could knock it off, then you'd do a Spencer Davis – 'Keep On Running.' A hit record in the Sixties. Ever heard that one?

You probably haven't.

Well, that's something you've learnt today, anyhow.

You might think it's cruel. I would, today. To do that to an old person who'd suffered, whose children or grandchildren might have gone to the war and not come back? But if you could do it, hit them on the back of the head, you figured: it wouldn't hurt them much. They'd yell, —Oh you cheeky buggers! A bit of profanity off the old lady. You'd get away, yelling back, —Oh piss off you old swine! And then you'd run away.

But then if you were unlucky: —I'll tell my bleedin' son about you! *I know who you are!* You're Stan Kelly's son!

And if you heard your name, you knew you'd made a mistake. And if they caught you, they'd give you a crack. Which perhaps you deserved.

You know...I remember one of the fights I was in, with two brothers. One was about twelve, the other was ten. The argument was me and the ten-year-old, but the bigger brother came over and hit me – gave me a right crack. And of course, my Dad was just coming out of the house. he asked what happened. —He bleeding hit me!

—Who?

—Him, but he's bigger than me, Dad!

But Dad told me, —Just run up and try to hit him as hard as you can. And if you can't, just kick him on his ankles. But don't walk away. Have a go at him, otherwise they'll do it again and know they can get away with it. You've got to show a bit of resistance. Run up and *hit him!*

Well, I ran up and hit him. It didn't always land where it should do. And then he pushed me off. Dad called out:

—Kick him! And if not, run away as fast as you bleeding can! But don't run back to me...

My Dad would fight anybody, you know. I say that in a good way. He was a wonderful human being, my Dad. He would never allow you to swear in front of an old person. He'd say, — No no, we don't need any of that *farmyard.* That's what we used to call it.

Dad had a good job, compared with other people. He worked for Dunlop's, and he made a lot of money off his expenses. He'd go all over the country – back to Ireland as well. One time, he was working in Middlesborough, a coal-mining district. And he'd won on the football coupon – a bit like the Lotto. You could pick out ten results, ten to win. You'd take the easiest, what you thought were certainties. And if they came up, it was a lot of money. Say your wages were £5 a week – well, Dad won over £70. And remember, you could get a beer for a penny, and a pack of cigarettes for less than sixpence. So it was a lot of money.

(I'll tell you how much it was: when he came home we bought an expensive bedroom suite. Beautiful – too good for us, really, since the rest of the furniture didn't match up. You had one thing laughing at the other. But at least he could always put his two suits and two coats in the wardrobe.)

Anyhow, Dad bought everybody in the pub in Middlesborough a beer, and bought everyone outside, who smoked, a packet of cigarettes. Every one of them. And when he had to leave – the job was finished – he had a last drink, bought them a drink, and started to leave. And the lads that were in there said, —Oh no you don't, hold on a minute.

They carried him out of the pub on their shoulders.

They carried him to the train station and said, —Don't forget to come back.

He'd always cry when he told me about it... —To see them, son, they didn't have a *meal*. They didn't have decent shoes, couldn't go anywhere. A good meal would've killed them.

He said it was so hard to see that.

It's a hard thing to remember, as well, Dad telling me that story. But I'm grateful that I still can.

I watched *Hobson's Choice* recently. I tell you, I was young again, watching it. I can't express in words how I felt – you had Sir John Mills, from *Great Expectations*; his daughter is Hayley

Mills. Charles Laughton was the main star. I remember the woman in the lead, Brenda de Banzie, how beautiful she was. A marvelous movie, but it's more than a movie to me.

It shows you the whole neighbourhood where I used to live. It's about a shoe shop. A comedy. Charles Laughton, a piss-head, owns the place. Beautiful shoes. He has two people working for him in the cellar, making shoes, doing repairs. In his previous years he'd done it himself, I suppose. His daughter manages the business; the other two daughters, he wants them to marry local businessmen. The older sister takes care of the house, she's taken the place of his wife, who's passed away years ago. He's very…conformist. Of his era. Of course he has well-made winter boots on.

Now, his eldest daughter is sick of him going out every lunchtime and coming back pissed out of his head, expecting to have lunch, lying down, going out of a night after she makes dinner, and expecting her to handle the shop. Going into the till and taking out half a crown, a lot of money, every night before he went out. Pissing away all the profits. Now, John Mills – his inferior, though he's the best shoemaker – he's in the cellar. The daughter calls him up. She says, Now look here. The main woman in town, Lady So-and-so, your shoes are the only ones she'll wear. You've got a bright future. So come up now into the room.

He says: What do you mean? Where you *live?* You want me to come into the *parlour?* But the master's not here, I can't do that…

Come in here! she says. He asks if he's done something wrong. She says, No, of course not – I'm going to meet you in the park on Sunday, so *put your best suit on,* because I've chosen you as my future husband.

By gum! He can't believe her. It's impossible – that's the disparity between the lower class and the people with a few bob. It's not a matter of intelligence; he's a great craftsman, after all.

She tells her father she's going for this walk, with John Mills. You're *what?* You're too old to get married, you're *thirty* years of age!

Well, she's made her decision. She's got plans.

Honestly, I could recite the whole film.

Of course John Mills does become successful. It's a movie, after all. They get married, and now the store owner's got no one to cook for him – the other two daughters have no idea.

So one day Laughton's walking home – of course they all live in the same street – and he falls down a chute into some corn. So at least he's got a soft landing. He finishes up asleep, and he's discovered by someone who wants to marry one of his younger daughters. And they decide to sue him. Well, one thing leads to another. No matter.

It's only a movie, I know. But the world it portrays...that's Lancashire. Watching it on television, I'm *there*. When I was a boy during the war, people in Lancashire would say to me, — And what's *your* name? I'd tell them, and they'd say: —Well by gum, he's from the big city, he is. That's what they'd say.

I think I've mentioned elsewhere a trip to Stonyhurst that I took years later. I was with Bob Burrows, I think. I said to Bob, —Let's have a drink at this hotel. It wasn't as expensive as Harrod's, and we had a few quid on us. We ordered tea, and the lad who came was from Wigan. Very obvious in the way he spoke. —Anything else you'd like, sir? Some lovely crumb cake here, and it's made by *local* people. Good price for you!

I asked where he was from. —Oh, I'm from Manchester.

I said, —*I'm* from Manchester, you're not from Manchester!

He said, —I live a little bit out that way. Ramsbottom.

—Well that's *Lancashire*, really.

—Well if you don't come from Manchester, you come from, say, Ramsbottom...some of 'em that come in here, some right toffee-nosed bastards (he said to us), they stick their nose up at you.

I told him I wouldn't do that. —You're from Ramsbottom? Nothing wrong with that, because *I* used to do your job.

Anyhow, I gave him £5 tip. The tea was only about a pound. It was a lot of money. He said, —You want change? I told him no. —You've give me five pounds here!

—It's for you. Get your shoes mended.

He looked down at his shoes, a bit offended. —I don't bleedin' need them mended!

I said, —Well, it's for you.

—What, have you won the pools?

And I said that I was just glad to meet him.

Because I was him. That was me.

I thought of him going home, and his day would be made. His *week*. Whatever happened, he would be floating on a cloud.

And I've been there. I was there when I married Cata. She said we'd have the wedding reception at the yacht club, and I thought, *Christ, that'll be a change.* I can still remember coming off the ship, working with the lads from Liverpool: —Bleeding hell, Wally, you've done well. Has she got a few bob?

—More than me, I'd say.

—You marrying for money?

But I wasn't.

My roommate Teddy Cochran, on the ship, he loved Cata. He'd scold me: *Don't forget you're married, you...* She used to come onboard the ship to visit, and they'd fawn over her. They'd never seen someone like her. Neither had I.

During the war, if you were from the city, it was looked on as...well, people were naive, and they'd look at you a bit funny, thinking you had money. But it's been leveled out now, in a way. The mentality that was prevalent in those years, the 'have-nots.' If your shoes went wrong, you'd have them mended. If your socks had holes, you'd have them darned. Your laundry done every week – but you'd do it yourself. If your house was painted, *you* did it – if it was painted at all, mind you.

I don't mean to talk in circles. There's something I'm trying to say, but it's difficult.

My best pal when I was young, during the evacuation, was a black boy named Peter King, from Trinidad. Now, Peter saved my life when I fell in the Hodder River. I was hurt when I fell, and he got me out. (I've never been much of a swimmer, as I mentioned.) Peter went on to fight for the British boxing title. Another pal of mine was Albert Scanlon. We'd go down to Lee Street baths with no ball of our own and play soccer together, before the war ended. Albert played for Manchester United and England, and the week he was buried, United had a minute's silence for him. Silence.

And Billy Blower was my pal, who became David Wade, and played a command performance for the Queen.

Peter King's brother Joey, he won the Carroll Levis competition on television.

These are kids who had to put cardboard in their shoes. We had no underwear. I think of where we came from, my God – or rather, 'By gum, you did well...'

The lady of the shop turns around and says, —I'm going to marry you, because I know you've got a future. You'll be the best cobbler in England... And in the end, John Mills has to confront his father-in-law: —Now look here, if you want me to take to take over the business...

—Take over *my* business? Who do you think you are...?

But he says to Charles Laughton, —I'm the best thing that's ever happened to you, you're losing all your sales, and I'll make you a joint partner.

Laughton can't believe it. —Joint partner?

—If you'll listen to my demands.

—*Your demands?!* Who do you think you're talking to?

But he had to say it, you see. Or he'd have nothing.

When I was young, I was more conscious of my appearance than anyone else around. I'd get compliments just walking down the street, which was a lovely feeling – not the compliments, mind you, the feeling of looking that way, of looking like where you came from and like something else.

I remember Grandma told me once, —You've got a bright future. Remember your manners; wash your hands; keep your shoes clean. If you're wearing your clogs, make sure you knock the snow off. Remember to be honest. And if you're honest you'll get through.

I let her down by becoming a thief. But I felt I had no choice.

I hope I made up for it eventually.

When I first came back from Africa, after working on the ship, all the guys who used to sit there in the railway station waiting, without a dime to their names – I used to give them a pound each, so they could buy soup. A meal. I just *loved* doing it, and I could afford to, because I was making money on the side, selling bottles of rum, my fifty cigars, aftershave lotions... I'd bring two suitcases back with me, and if we arrived in the middle of the night and the customs people weren't around, I could get through customs without paying, and I'd make a week's wages – on *each* suitcase. I couldn't afford to do that later on, because life had leveled out – I became a father and so on, with real responsibilities.

My Dad died a few years before my sons were born. He would have adored them. (My eldest son is named after my Dad, like I am; my youngest is named after Cata's father, Philip.)

I think of the men in the pub carrying Dad to the train station on their shoulders, calling out to him, *Don't forget to come back*. And I think of Dad telling me that story and crying.

Honestly, I don't remember the name of John Mills's character in the movie. But do you know, I remember *being* him. I really do:

You mean, you want me to come into the *parlour?*

Me?

CHAPTER 4

After the war

After the war I became a thief.

I promise to tell you about it, as they say on TV, 'after these messages.' First I want to talk a little more about our life at that time.

As I've said before, we didn't have hot water in our houses; I imagine the list of things we *didn't* have is longer than the list of things we *did*.

On a Monday, if you went to school, and if you owned a tennis ball, that was the ball you'd play *soccer* with. Where kids have indoor soccer now, and they'll bounce the ball off the wall, that's how we'd play outside, bouncing the ball off the school or the building next door. You had to be careful of windows on the back of the school, of course. But you had no choice – it's not as if there was a grass field to play on. You had to sneak across the city to play on grass. Where my eldest son lives in Massachusetts, every house in the city is within a few minutes' walk of a park. And of course Ellicottville, where I live now, is more trees and deer than people – like Stonyhurst. But in the city we didn't have any of that.

Everything had changed for me during the evacuation. Except for the occasional bit of flying roof slate or giant owl, I was off in paradise.

And it all changed again when we came back.

The city was in ruins, you see. We'd been bombed out of our home three times; the family who'd lived across from us on Chatham St, the Muirheads, whom we used to take baths with, had been killed; Old Trafford had been bombed, the whole city had been transformed. Thousands of people were dead. It would be years before the city was 'normal' again.

Being there amidst the ruins was one of the most magical feelings I've ever experienced.

That may be hard to understand, but it's true.

After living on a country lane with five cottages, it was back to city life: dozens of houses on each side of the street. You'd just have an alley between houses at the back, about two and a half yards wide.

It's hard to imagine now: you had to boil the water for a bath. There was no electricity, only gas. The main light would be on the mantle, and it's not as if you could have it on all day. In the parlour, you'd have to take a candle to have light – though some people had paraffin lamps. You don't think it's much, to switch on an overhead light when you walk into a room. But back then it would have been a miracle.

You didn't see anybody that was well off; anyone you knew was in the same boat, unless they had a shop – like Smoky Bacon's parents, who even had a car, I think. You'd go to school all week; then Friday thru Sunday there would be movies on at the picture house, like a small miracle.

Now, you had ration books for food and clothes, and a special page for chocolate powder, which they'd sell without a stamp, I don't know why. We'd get soap, and the same soap you'd wash with, you'd also use for laundry. There were no laundry machines in your home, of course; women would go to the launderette, pay so much to get in, and then scrub their own clothes. Some women would take laundry for others who couldn't do it, as a way of making a bit of extra money.

At school on a Monday, the nuns – who weren't our teachers – would do the first couple of hours visiting, asking whether we'd gone to church on Sunday and so forth. Well, I didn't always go. Neither did most of us, the reason being that church was two miles away! And we were walking, of course. If it was raining, it's not as though you had a cap; you'd put an old newspaper on the top of your head and off you went. No offense to Father Mierzwa, but I'm sorry – I was better off staying home.

The handy bit, though, was you'd save the newspaper to light the fire later: newspaper in the fire grate, then firewood, then coal, if you had it to spare. One more reason to stay home on a Sunday, save it getting wet in the first place.

We used to have a tin bath occasionally, perhaps three feet long, a foot or two wide. You'd have a bath in front of the fire. Dad and me, on different nights we'd have the bath in front of the fire, and my sister would bathe when she wanted to. And a 'mobile bath unit' would come to the school, twice a week I think, and stay late afterward. They'd supply towels and everything. Done by the government.

Tide marks all around on Mondays, so you knew which families were saving hot water.

For a haircut, you'd just get a 'bowl cut': put a basin on top of your head, shave the base of your head, then clippers on top. We used to have a lot of lice. To get rid of them they'd use liquid paraffin, same as you'd use in a lamp.

The lice had more to eat than we did, which is only fair – they had more mouths to feed.

I can't moan about it though. The wartime spirit still prevailed.

I remember the McDonoughs, Kellys, Mannions, Lyonses, Buckleys – large families with several kids, and many of them would wear navy or army uniforms together. They'd gone off to join the British army, and you'd read about them in the local paper: the pride of England.

Everyone did what they could; sometimes they had no choice. My father worked in rubber, at Dunlop's down by Trafford Park, in an area where munitions were being manufactured. Lord Haw-Haw, the German radio propagandist, would mention it on his broadcasts. —*Oh, we're coming down to see about Dunlop's,* he'd say. They were coming for all of us, we were in it together, but he was talking about my *dad*. I hated him.

Near Dunlop's was Old Trafford, where United would play; when the Germans bombed it in 1941, an incendiary bomb landed in the middle of the pitch. That district was full of factories – at Dunlop's they'd make barrage balloons and plane wheels. And bladders for soccer balls, actually, not that *we* ever got one out of it.

The government ask us to return any kind of tins and cans, to put them in a disposal for collection. They needed the metal. Can you imagine, the Queen asking for old cans? And so you gave, if you had any.

In American movies we'd see them taking up collections of money and so forth, which was well and good for them. But we didn't have *money* – those who did, needed it just to keep their cars running. I remember during the Blitz, a bomb dropped outside Joe Purcelli's on Cambridge Street but didn't go off. It was famous in the city. People would walk by and put a farthing in – but *not* a dime, as that was a lot of money. You see? You gave what you could, and not a penny more.

If you worked on munitions like my dad, you had to be up at six in the morning to catch the bus to Trafford Park. During the war it was busier than Piccadilly; buses ran 24 hours a day. If Dad missed the bus, he'd come back home and get his bike as a last resort. That wasn't about getting there to work, really – if you were late for a munitions job, they might accuse you of being a saboteur.

People who didn't go into the forces could work as air raid wardens if they liked. There was one named Jonty Moffett – he was about 5'2", and I never saw him dressed in anything but a raincoat and a hat. He had an eighteen-foot cane made of bamboo for tapping on top-floor windows. He'd go up and down the street, and he made a decent amount of money doing it. (Mind you, not many people wanted the job.) And of course, most of the windows were broken anyway by the end of the war. Even if the bomb didn't hit you, you might wake up at night to shattered glass. And if you slept in the parlour, as my mum did when she was ill, the glass could even come on to the bed.

I never realized, until years after I left, just how close Stonyhurst was to Stirk House, where I worked as an adult. When it comes to distances and directions, I'm completely useless. North, west? Nothing. I don't have that map in my mind. Same with dates – American vacations, holidays? No recollection at all. President's Day? You must be joking.

But when it comes to remembering childhood...

It was so exciting for me. I was in a world of my own. A dreamworld. I was so happy to be alive, as a child – I had black curly hair; I'd clean my teeth, even though there was no toothpaste (I'd use soot and salt and water). I did lose a few teeth along the way, but only ever from the back, so no great loss. I was always conscious of being clean: clean hands and nails, a handkerchief. Good manners, not a hair out of order.

I was what you might call...phony, in a way. I tried to be what I wasn't, and so I wasn't what I tried to be. But that was who I am. I tended to my appearance because I could.

During the evacuation I'd talk too much. (I'm a bit more reserved now; you start to realize there's no point conversing with *some* people.)

Certain things make me uncomfortable, ever since I was a child. Obesity, for instance: I sympathize with women who've had children, say, who naturally put on weight. That's life. But I think about what it meant to have enough food... For lunch at school, some of us would have jam, you see, but some would have bread with sugar and honey all together. The families that piled sweets onto their bread would be noticeably fatter than the rest of us. Everyone else was skinny. It felt like they were getting away with something.

The same with body odours. If somebody smokes and we're walking down the street, that I can't stand either. In a café, certainly, I understand that. But walking down the street: no. I'm trying to give you an idea of who I am and how I think. When you grow up with no food, no bath, and certain things remind you of what you *don't* have—

I know it's not fair, but I feel how I feel.

We didn't have to go to school, so obviously you'd have kids playing outside. We'd play soccer together, swing from a rope on a lamppost, play pitch & toss with ha'pennies if we had them. There were grates in the walls, a foot across, with a lip at the bottom, and you'd toss coins into them (which would be extricated afterward, of course).

Those were the small things that made up our life. The war is history, and the rest is just our life.

Even when school was on, we'd play truant, swim in the canals. We'd go to bakers' shops, big stores, with cakes 15" off the floor on the bottom shelf, under a glass partition. Myself and a chap called Haddocks were able – we were so small – to climb underneath on our bellies or backs, come to the other side of the counter, put our hands up quickly, and steal a couple of cakes. Back down on the floor quick and come out underneath – providing the lady at the counter had turned her back, of course.

It was only Haddocks and me could do that. Everyone else was too big.

After coming back from Stonyhurst I was 10, 12 years old – I could look after children. Some of the younger parents would like to go out and have a drink, which may only have meant walking 200 yards. It would be nice for the husband and wife to get out and do that. So I'd look after the children, make sure they didn't cry, and if they did, worse comes to worst, I could run to the pub for their parents. If they were old enough, I'd read stories to them. The kids, I mean.

We had our *Champion*, the *Rover*, the *Hotspur*, the *Wizard*, and the *Adventurer*. We called them 'comics.' I'm not joking when I say they were the most important thing in the world. A lot of people structure their lives around the Bible; I've never read it in my life, and have no intentions of doing so. A lot of people have asked me since I came to America, —Have you ever read the Bible?

I say no, and never enlarge on it. Honestly, who wants to get into a conversation about the Bible? But show me a *Rover*, a *Champion*, and I'll thank the good Lord.

When I got my *Champion* during the war, nothing in the world, not even the movies, compared to reading them. It was your own imagination. And I lived in a dreamworld. Well, you had to, didn't you?

I only went to school for four years in the aftermath of war, from 11-15 – I was off playing truant for most of that last year and forging passes for the lads, which is why I was expelled. So the *movies* educated me instead: I only found out who President Lincoln was through a movie. You had the *Pathé News* to keep you up to date, though most of it was propaganda, I suppose.

And we could use the monthly food coupons for sweets! To be able to go to the movies with a bar of chocolate was like...living in springtime, a vacation. I can't explain it. And it would be *packed*, you know. They'd be queueing up for ages, so crowded you couldn't get in, and everyone had *walked* there...

We were still going through it every day, rebuilding, but we didn't have to dwell on it all the time.

After the war, things got built back up again, of course, but it took a long time, so for instance I ended up going to a Protestant school. Things didn't go back to normal just because the bombing stopped. It was the same but different, all at once. But there's different sorts of different, you might say. When I went to Tokyo in 1953, parts of the country still hadn't been rebuilt. I went to one of the cities where the Americans dropped the A-bomb, I can't remember which. I took a coach or a train. Parts of the city were still completely devastated. I remember seeing a woman with what looked like two noses, one protruding from the side of her face.

It was the most horrible thing I'd ever seen. But all the same, I felt as if Japan had been rebuilt more quickly than England. Their country had been demolished, so they were starting from scratch, in a way; we had bits and pieces strewn about, and built on those. The government built utility homes – they were improvising, just like we were – and years later, you had people still living in the prefab homes they'd been given...

I know how lucky we were, my family. Dad knew as well.

On one occasion Dad was working for a lord, and he had to go in through the back door – a labourer wouldn't be allowed through the front – which meant passing through the wine cellar. He told us all about it, said it was something to see. Of course they treated him like a piece of shit. The lord of the house wouldn't speak to Dad directly; he sent a servant down to deal with him, order him around. I remember my father saying once that the house took a direct hit from a bomb. —I remember *that* bastard, he said. But then he added: —I hope he wasn't in it.

You see, when the bombers came to Manchester, sometimes Spitfires came up in time to chase after them. If they were going away from the main targets, they'd drop their bombs anywhere. May as well. And one of them fell on the house my father had worked in. They were probably in the cellar.

I'm sure they were fine.

That was how it was with the aristocracy, and still is. The queen, the lords – you know they're there, but you can't reach them. They'd have houses with thousands of acres of land; you'd go through the gate, at the perimeter of their land, you may be traveling another two miles. You couldn't even *see* them.

All the same, Dad hoped that nothing had happened to the lord he'd worked for, and he meant it.

That's who *he* was.

You couldn't have a proper football league during the war. You might have a couple of players from Manchester United working in Southampton, say, so they'd play for different teams there – Tom Finney played for Preston North End, one of the greatest we ever had. He was in the Army with Ernie Horton, a friend of my dad's, and if they were in Liverpool, they'd play for Liverpool. You wouldn't worry too much about who was on which team, contracts and that – there were other things to worry about. Toward the end of the war, I saw Accrington Stanley play in a cup tie at Clitheroe. They won 4-3. I don't know who they played, but I know that at that time, it was the greatest match I'd seen in my life.

United didn't play at Old Trafford; they played at Maine Road, City's venue, because Old Trafford took a direct hit from a bomb. It destroyed everything around it. So every week, City or United played at Maine Road. When it came to the cup ties in 1948, in the aftermath, United won the FA Cup, beating Blackpool 4-2. United played all their games away, as they had no ground of their own to play on. I went to see United play at...Huddersfield, if I remember rightly, and beat Charlton Athletic 2-0, against a famous goalkeeper named Sam Bartram.

I can't even remember how old I was when I left my parents and my home in Manchester. But I remember Sam Bartram at Huddersfield.

After that, I think United had to play at Villa Park. Not home yet – there wasn't yet a home to return to.

It felt that way sometimes, I suppose.

I think it should be in the record books: for a team to win the FA Cup without ever playing at home? But United were put in that position, and won every game, and beat Blackpool 4-2 to win the Cup. In those days Stanley Matthews played for Blackpool on the right wing, like Tom Finney. During the war Matthews was the big name. I thought Finney was a better player, as a lot of them were frightened of *touching* Matthews, in case they hurt his legs – he was getting on. (He got on so well he became *Sir* Stanley Matthews, later. I wonder if he had a wine cellar of his own.) When United beat Blackpool, it was a bit of a shock.

But this was the right sort of shock for a change, especially for us. My Uncle Freddie worked for Harry Gold, the bookie, and they backed My Love in the derby in 1948 (Ray Johnson riding, the Australian jockey), which Uncle Freddie had a tip for – well, they backed United the same year, the year they won the cup. They weren't expected to win. And all the money that Unkie and Harry Gold had, they put on United.

Thousands and thousands of pounds. Most of it was Harry Gold's, of course, but Unkie had something going on the side. You had My Love at 8-1, though Unkie got the tip at 16-1, and United over Blackpool to win the Cup, 4-2. And they cleaned up on everyone betting *against* them as well.

That was a good year. Well: a hard year, a few hard years, but a couple of very good days that made the next years easier.

Amy, Margaret, and I went to Ireland on vacation that year, and stayed at the guest house of a champion runner named Miller in Bray, County Wicklowe. Unkie paid – and left them a lot of money later on. They were able to buy houses when they got married; so did their brother Teddy. That was in the late 50s or early 60s. Even then, there was money in their family to go around – that's how well Unkie did in 1948.

That's the world I lived in, back then. You had to keep moving, find ways to get by. When I worked in Oxford St at Tootal's, I could cut up pieces of white paper to use as betting slips, and take them down to Unkie, five minutes away. Unkie would give me five shillings each week for the papers. So I made a bit. And I sold firewood during the war, delivered newspapers, looked after children, ran errands, went for coal... I always made a bit of money, so I could afford to buy handkerchiefs, which my other friends never had. I remember that well, because sometimes they came in quite handy.

One particular boy, Peter Lynch, we were playing in the old York Street school, Saint Augustine's, which was demolished by a land mine during the war. The 'playground' was concrete. Sometimes of a night we'd go play soccer there, mostly with a tennis ball. One night he was going for the ball off the wall, ran into a section of metal windowframe, and basically severed his nose. I was the only one that had a handkerchief for him.

Peter Lynch came to a bad end, later, though I don't wish to talk about that. He was a pal of Frankie Croker's, who went to Korea with me, and who'd go to the railway stations and steal unattended suitcases. He'd see a nice one that matched his, a substitute full of newspapers or rags, and switch the two. Lynch, Croker, and David Broomhead were school pals. Lynch wasn't part of *our* gang, though. He swapped in after I swapped out, you might say.

Unkie knew I was getting involved with the wrong people. He had people come into where he was working, when Dad was away, and they'd tell him: —That Wally lad's going to get into trouble. Which was quite right.

So Unkie took me to live with him. His son Teddy was older than me, and different from me; I loved Teddy very dearly, like he was my brother, which he was in a way, during the war. Unkie said I was 'nippy': fast on my feet, and wise in a way. Able to get by on the street, in the city; understanding what the racetrack was, signaling even money. (I worked as a 'tic-tac,' signaling to bettors for the bookmakers. I suppose that's *one* way of being wise, anyhow.)

I didn't go to school much, but I learned some things along the way. One day I went to the racecourse at Castle Hurwell, where Unkie was working. I'd won £7, quite a lot of money, and had taken a day off work to have a tooth out, but they took out the wrong tooth. (The war changed so many things, but I don't think English dentistry was one of them.) I was working for Morreau Spiegelberg, in Deansgate – that's where I met Malcolm Tierney, the movie actor, who was friends with Ian McShane, of *Lovejoy*. (And McShane's dad played for United, on the right wing. I've seen enough of the world to know it's *not* small, but it still feels that way at times.) Anyhow, Unkie put £50 on a horse, and I figured I may as well put a pound on. We both lost. No harm done, I thought.

Unkie pulled me to one side. —What are you doing here? he said. —Same as you, losing a pound, I said.

—No, I've not lost anything, he responded. I'm working for the bookie, to pull the mugs in.

—You've bleedin' pulled *me* in, never mind the 'mugs!'

—Then you've been educated today, he said.

I think Unkie saw me as being a little bit like what he wanted for his son – a bit lively. Well, he got his wish, in a way. I didn't join the family business; I couldn't be a bookie (no good with numbers) and I grew too tall to be a jockey.

So I became a thief instead.

CHAPTER 5

A little thief

Once upon a time, I was a thief. I hope that surprises you to learn.

I sometimes say it was *magical* coming back to Manchester. The city didn't look quite like a city – not like *our* city, I mean. Instead of new buildings, you had new stones, new holes, new places to explore.

And you could change it, you see. If you were light on your feet, there was a chance to move about, to make a bit of a mark. As kids we were free in a way, and we loved it.

When I was young the fellows in the gangs would use me as a 'foil.' I was small and looked tidy, so they'd send me into the pharmacy, and when someone would ask for help at the desk, I'd put tablets of soap in my pocket and run off. When we did big stuff, like stealing cigarettes from passing trucks, I didn't get involved. But others in the gang would, and I'd take my share. I was already smoking by then.

In the bombed-out sections of the city, the houses still had wooden sections in them. The windows would have crowbars as levers to bring them up and down. Those came in handy: you'd cut the string off and take the bar with you, climb up the stairs – there were only two floors, you didn't have far to go – and smash the cupboards in with the bar, to get the wood. New hinges would fetch decent money at the hardware shop.

You'd prise the baseboards away from the wall with a knife, pull the floorboards up whole, and drop them down into the bottom floor through the holes you'd made. Now you'd come outside with the boards, put them on the steps outside, and jump on the center of the boards and *crack* them in half – to make them small enough to carry.

Once you've done your floorboards, you're taking the insides of the stairsteps. (To any young thieves who might be reading, some advice: it's important not to take the stairs out *before* going up and down.) You'd also get the doors, upstairs and down. If you'd already taken the upstairs floorboards, you could just drop the doors through the same holes in the floor.

We'd use sacks to carry wood. We'd use a wagon on a string, sometimes with two or three wheels if that was all we had. We'd put two boards on top, and then we could stack everything else on top of the boards. You could do more work that way. I'd take them to my customers. They trusted me, because I'd do things like take the nails out of the wood before bringing it by.

Once you had all the cupboards in the house, you could take the windowframes as well – and pick up spare crowbars for the *next* job.

I know, I know: those weren't our things to take. But there's no sense letting an *entire house* go to waste, is there?

When Dad was away, I ran with a gang. We'd jump on the back of Carter Paterson's trucks, break the lock on the door, and steal the cartons of cigarettes inside. Whole cartons! You can't blame me for taking up smoking when we're getting whole cartons for free.

There was a company that did food, next door to Dunlop's; they had a conveyor belt on the inside of the building, and one night we went down there, took the wooden paneling off the outside wall, and stuck something next to the conveyor belt. And the food started coming out the side of the building! We'd get tins of salmon, loads of food...it was stealing. Then we left it as it was, dashed away.

That night we had two bags full of food. I was with two lads, Broomhead and Croker. I was stood between the two of them, and we heard a shout: —Ay ay, stop that! It was a policeman. Well, dealing with police is all part of the job, isn't it. But then I heard two **bangs**, like objects hitting the ground, one on my left, one on my right. I look around and Croker and Broomhead are gone, just like that, and there are two food bags on the ground beside me where they've dropped them and left me behind.

It's times like this when you begin to question your choices a bit.

I ran past the police officer as fast as you like, and *then* realized I was running toward the police station on Ormond Street, next to our church.

No one's perfect.

I turned left at an alley, with my back against the wall. The policeman ran past me, and I was *gone*. I ran as fast as I could, and didn't stop until I was sure I was clear.

I finished up in Timpley. That was *four miles* away, nowhere near where I lived. Do you remember the song I mentioned, 'Keep On Running'?

You *still* haven't heard it, have you.

Back to thieving: if we walked into the pharmacy to get soap, I'd be the one to approach the person at the counter...I had a white handkerchief and my hair combed and clean, nicely dressed. These weren't the days right after the war when I had cardboard in my shoes and no underwear – those days had gone. That's when I sold firewood, did a newspaper round, sold programs for City. (United used their soccer ground, because a land mine had destroyed the field at Old Trafford.)

I was a well-dressed little thief for a few years after the war. But once I left and went to Withington, I stopped all that. I had to live there. The lads in the gang, we all went our separate ways.

At school, Broomhead sat on one side of me and Croker on the other. Frankie Croker wore his hair crewcut on the top, and straight down on the sides, as though he had a box on his head. He became a *professional* thief.

When I volunteered for Korea, only two privates out of five thousand in the battalion went away on the ship. I was one of them. And when we got on the ship at Liverpool, who do I see on the ship but...Croker. He's in an engineers unit. I was in the Ordnance Corps, doing supplies. I also bumped into Bob Martin, who went into school nearby us, on Webster St. Their team had two black players, the Johnsons – very good players. The only two black boys I knew in school. Bob and I were pally on ship. He was in the Ordnance Corps in a different unit, also going to Korea.

I'd see Croker from time to time. You had two thousand men going over, in different units: the King's Own, the Duke of Wellington's, the Black Watch. I'd started playing cards – blackjack. I did quite well. Most of the lads playing were Scottish. You can easily end up in a fight with a Scots guy, especially the Black Watch. Great people to be friends with, though. I'd go by and they'd shout out: —Dutch! You having a game?

I won quite a lot of money. It was a five-week trip. So now I bump into Croker. He mentions a guy selling raffle tickets: a basket of fruit, cigarettes. We only made a pound a week, so that was a nice prize. (At one stage I was winning twelve quid on cards, so that wasn't bad either.) Now, Croker's with me, and said, —Well, I'll have a couple of tickets. And I bought one for Croker as well.

—Well give it me, he said.

—No, no, I said. —I'm not giving you the *ticket;* if you win you'll take the prize for yourself. I'll be there when they draw the raffle, you won't.

He moaned at me a bit. Then before the raffle started, he moaned some more: —You've not bought *me* a ticket, you've not *given* me the ticket, how can you say you've give me a ticket if you've not give me the ticket?

He had a point. —*Here's* the bleeding ticket, then.

And of course he won the raffle. I had to get it off him, going from one end of the ship to the other to get the prize. Fruit and cigarettes! Five weeks' wages, the swine.

So some time passes, we go to Korea and Japan, and I get demobbed. I'm in England with Smoky Bacon. We used to write to each other. He was a month before me, in Trieste. He wrote to me: *Wait while you get home. They're wearing white socks and yellow socks, Elvis Presley's big, the back of the jackets is just one piece, and the lapels don't match the jackets.*

I wrote back, —*Not me, baby.*

So we're back in England. Smoky's got a pub he goes to, where you can always get a game and a bit of entertainment. We're there on a Sunday. You'd always get a few people outside, talking about United and whatever. Now, you remember I mentioned the grate in front of the houses, where you'd drop the coal, in front of the door? Well, they had one in front of the pub, larger than the one in front of a house, big enough for a man to crawl into.

We're stood in front of the pub. And we see the grate come up, pushed to one side. And who do you think climbs out of the hole?

It's only Croker. He's just robbed the pub. He stands up, covered in coal, holding the money from the gas meter. Joe Bacon, Smoky's father, came out with some colleagues and gave him a good hiding.

That was the last I saw of Croker. The next thing I heard about him, he was going to railway stations, and he'd walk by and pick up someone's case and walk off. Well, they caught him, and I believe they put him away for a few years.

That was that.

The other fellow in the gang, whose name I won't mention, he finished up having some problems with a prostitute, over payment. And he strangled her. I didn't know about it until years later.

I think about the things I've done and I'm grateful. And then I think about the things I've *not* done, the ways I might have ended up, and I'm grateful all over again.

The best thing about being a little thief, in my experience, is meeting other little thieves.

Harold Grimsley, the cock of the school – 'Grimmo' to me – was in one of the gangs. Grimmo was my best pal for quite a while; I adored him. He was the image of James Cagney, only harder than Cagney: he'd fight anyone, within reason, no matter how big they were. The only fight he ever *lost* was against quite a bright fellow, actually, 6'2" where Harold was about 5'4". The big lad kept sticking his left out. Harold couldn't reach him! The other lad hit him, 1—2—3, and Harold quickly said, —OK, you win. That's enough.

Sensible move, really. If he could have won, he'd have gone back at him until he did. He was jumped by a gang once, they all got on top of him and gave him a right kick, his eyes were swollen out to here, they kicked his teeth. But *later*, he picked them all off one by one. The lot of them. Inbetween the Lyonses and the Buckleys, he sorted everybody out.

Grimmo was a smashing fellow. I thought the world of him, and he always respected me. Instead of 'Wally,' he'd call me *Walter* – with an air to it, what with me living in Withington and having a white handkerchief and so forth.

Grimmo died a few years ago. Of the Lloyds Celtic soccer team, only a couple of us are left. Arthur had a stroke years ago, I gather; Brian passed away recently. Johnny Moores is still with us; I phone him quite regularly.

Johnny lived in the next street over from us, Rosamund Street. A big family. The McElroys were there too, and the Kellys (different from the Frank Kellys on the other side). I was in love with Johnny's sister Maureen. She was the same age as me, but completely ignored me. I loved the way she looked after her sisters. Josephine, her younger sister, was also very beautiful. I liked her, but that was more of a sensuous matter, when she got older. Maureen I was infatuated with. Oh well.

Johnny was my best pal for a while too. His family was Irish – still are, actually. His father was a painter. His mother passed away when he was young, like mine; he grew up with his stepmother. We had something in common there.

Johnny's father used to call me in for a cup of cocoa. It was cheap – you'd have it if you didn't have tea. The Moores actually had cups to spare, since they had a lot of kids. They'd always respect me. When my mum died, Johnny took care of me, consoled me. The same with Grimmo – Grimmo would hit you if you made a mistake, or if he was in a bad mood, especially after a soccer game. He'd bleeding rip you to pieces verbally. But with my mum dying, he didn't do that. He was humane like that. (If I'd have been playing *against* him, he'd have kicked me anyhow.)

When he was married, we had a bachelor party, a meetup in the pub. (You paid for your own bleeding beer, of course. Nobody bought you anything – this was 1955, I think.) The pub was the Stone Mason, down the street from the Ritz. Now, I'd gone to this party in a beautiful brown overcoat of my dad's, single breasted, heavy and expensive. On the way back, I had a mile and a half walk. I had to pass Paulden's next to Cambridge St and Oxford Rd. They had an open space, under an awning, where you'd have prostitutes gathering. (Why do I have it in mind that Cary Grant's wife owned the place?) There was a pub on the opposite corner, with three guys picking on another fellow. Punching him. When I came up to the corner, one of them shouted: —Ay ay, here's one here!

And they started coming after *me*. Well, I ran around the corner. But I had this bleeding big heavy overcoat on, weighing me down. (On the other hand, they'd been drinking.) One of them was faster than the others and kept chasing me, but I was fastest of all, younger than them; these fellows were in their thirties or forties. So I outpaced him, and lasted. But when I got home, I was in a bit of a mess.

I couldn't speak. My dad said: —Wall, where were you?

I told him what had happened. Not surprisingly, he knew the pub. He said, —Come with me now. Just point them out to me. You don't have to go near them, just tell me which ones they are.

He wanted to go for them, there and then. My dad would fight anybody. But I didn't want to go. He asked me to describe them instead. I described the first one, and Dad said, —Oh, was the other one a smaller fellow? I said yes. —Don't worry about that, son. I'll see to them in the next couple of days.

And he did do. Dad caught them poncing – picking on someone for their money, threatening them. Three of them. But then, Dad's pal Ernie Horton was 6'4". Dad and Ernie sorted the other three men out.

The life of an English criminal, even just a small one, isn't complete without football.

Ernie Horton was the best player that Clynes's ever had. Albert Scanlon was the top left-winger in the area, and next to him was Dennis Jones. They both played with me for Stanford Albion in the early 50s. I can't remember if I played for Clynes's once or twice – as good as I was, or thought I was, I wasn't good enough for the team. I was a right winger. (Not politically, just on the field.)

We weren't bad, you know. A few of the lads from back home could really *play*. Grimmo was the school captain. Ernie Horton played for the Army, as captain, and played for Preston North End as an amateur, with the great Tom Finney – the best winger in Great Britain, in my day. And Billy Meredith – a pal of my dad's – he'd work down in the mines in the morning and play for United in the afternoon, in the 1920s and 30s. Stanley Matthews had the biggest name of all in the 40s, but he wasn't as good as Tom Finney. They played for England together, Matthews on the right wing and Finney on the left, out of position. Finney was the more accomplished player, and faced better competition as well.

It's a pleasure to remember all this, you know. I hope you don't mind me telling you.

We had a little guy play against us on Lloyds Celtic, named Pedlar Johnson. Good as Grimmo and I were, Pedlar was the best of all of us. And he was even smaller than me. Further down the street where he lived was a little chap named Arthur Boswell who did become a jockey. (We were all small, I suppose. Maybe it was the food.) Pedlar Johnson finished up playing for Fulham, actually, and Peter Phoenix played for Stockport County, and became quite well-known.

City and United used the same ground for a time, Maine Road. If the weather was good you'd walk – it was five miles, but you'd save the bus fare. It may sound pitiful, but then there might be fourteen of us walking together, and only one of us able to buy a program, which we'd all share.

Once you got to the ground, you'd go to the same spot every time. That was where *you* stood, and if someone else took your spot, you'd tell them to piss off.

I watched England play Scotland at Maine Road in 1955, with Stanley Matthews playing for England. There were 75,000 that day, and only the ones in the stands were sitting down, the ones with money – the *owners*. They used to let us in cheaper at Maine Road, us kids, but I was small enough to sneak under the bars anyhow. You'd come in from the back, and there would be *thousands* of people in front of you, between you and the game. But the men in the back would yell out, —Ay ay, we've got kids here!

And they'd *toss* you down toward the front of the crowd, passing you over people's heads, one to the other. You'd roll! It was jam-packed, so you'd never fall. There would be a steel bar keeping people in the stands at the front, with the crowd leaning on it – one on the left, one on the right. There were disasters in earlier years – in 1946 a disaster at Bolton where many people were crushed and died. I was there when Arsenal played City at Maine Road, 72,000 in the crowd. They'd throw us over the wall onto the ground to make room. There was real danger.

The world saw that at Hillsborough in 1989. I was out of the country by then.

City has a new ground, now, and United's ground was rebuilt after the war.

I love talking about the old players. I start to remember games, plays, trips to different parks, and I can practically see them in front of me, here and now.

I work as an official, for school games in Ellicottville – the oldest in New York State, I'm proud to say. And when I see the young players at the games, some of them are better than me, even at my best. I was very good at distributing the ball and positional playing, but I could never pull the ball out of the air like they can, chest the ball down, lob it, move with the same intelligence.

But I don't mind. I played for some great teams, saw some magnificent ones, and if I wanted, I could walk 200 yards from my house and there was Georgie Best, the greatest player I ever saw in my lifetime – and I've seen some players.

George Best asked my girlfriend for a date, once. But *he* never got a chance to meet *me*.

There's something unusual about these lads.

Peter King pulled me out of the river, saving my life. I was very grateful to him. When we were evacuated at Hurst Green, Peter lived with three spinsters, and they used him like a servant. Years later, Peter trained at the boxing club where I met Jimmy Hogan, one of the great coaches in Europe. Later on he fought another chap named Peter Waterman in London for the British lightweight title, and did well for himself.

Peter's brother Joe won the Carroll Levis television contest for Nat King Cole.

Billy Blower, my pal from Bark Street, was a comedian in a double act with a chap named Pat Dailey – a marvelous singer from Ireland. . Billy said to me once, —Will you come and watch the audition? I did. I told him, —Billy, doing impersonations you're not going to do too well.

Well, I'll never be a talent agent. Dailey and Wayne did a Martin & Lewis act and got big on television later.

Albert Scanlon was at Munich, and played for United and England. He was my pal too, playing together with Dennis Jones.

They were just kids from *nothing*, with tide marks on their necks the same as me. The standard of living that we had was *putrid*. But we were all in the same boat. Kids living around the corner, playing soccer with a tennis ball, or becoming thieves like Frank and me. When I think about what might have happened to me...

But we went places. You saw us in the strangest of places.

Billy Blower lived near Dad when I lived at Withington. I used to dress smartly, and people knew me since I'd sell dress lengths and get things made for people. I could make a bit of money that way. I wasn't a spiv; I tried to deal honestly with people. People liked me well enough. (Girls loved my black curly hair.)

One Sunday morning, Billy was coming down the street as I came out of the house. —Oh *Billy,* that jacket you're wearing! (Charcoal, tweed, a light chalk in it, double breasted.) —Can I try it on? We were the same size, it fit me like a glove. —Billy, this is too good for you.

—Well *you're* not bleeding getting it, that's for sure.

He said he'd been given it the previous night. He went to a party and mentioned to the girl he was with that he didn't have one. So she gave it to him. —But this is a lot of money! I said.

—Yeah, they've got a lot of money.

—Oh, what's her name?

—Well, the girl's name is Jackie Collins. Her sister's named Joan.

By the way – since this is my memoir, after all – I finished up going to see Billy at the cabaret, with a beautiful girl I'd been crazy about – I used to see her when I was coming home from work on the bus. One night she happened to sit next to me, I asked her on a date. She said she'd been engaged to a policeman and had just broken it off. I think he must have arrested her, as *I* never saw her in all that time. But here she was, single and on the bus, and she said yes to my offer. I took her out on a date, took her home, met her mother, we got on well. And then she said, —We've gotten back together.

She married the policeman.

Good luck to her.

CHAPTER 6

Odd jobs

The first job I ever had, not counting thieving or firewood rounds or helping Unkie rob the gamblers, was as an apprentice with J.F. Brooks, a French polishing shop with a little factory where they made furniture.

I only got the job by accident, the way you do.

About seven of us worked there. One chap was 6'4" but with his body bent out of shape. His name was David Gollop. He had a nice disposition, but people never treated him like a normal man, because of the way his body was formed. And he *wasn't* normal, was he? But he was a man all the same. I was only young. People would take liberties with him. I didn't know better – but some of them did.

We used to play a game with two ha'pennies and a sixpenny piece, pushing them on a board. You'd use one coin to hit another into a little goal at the end of the table. The foreman was the best player there. He always wore a light brown coat, and beating everybody at the game was a big part of his life. I was new, though – and I beat him. It didn't go down too well. I know that sounds silly, but it made a difference in the work.

They'd send me for errands and so forth, with me being young and small and a bit nippy.

They had an office in Deansgate; we were just the factory. The owner, Mr Brooks, had two sons a little older than me – I could tell who *they* were because they always wore suits. Mr Brooks wanted me to go in to the office and work as a salesperson. Fair enough.

Now, the rationing was on; at lunchtime you'd normally have tea with sugar and milk. They were able to get additional bits of food for the crew, as an allowance for the factory workers. But it appeared there was never any extra at *our* place. I asked the foreman, —Why do they not have tea with sugar?

—Shut up, they said.

And they gave me a tuppence raise in my wages, to make sure I didn't ask again.

Meaning the food was being taken by the family. Food was scarce then, even after the war, and you were only allowed so much. But you could have more if you didn't mind going around what was allowed, so to speak.

Anyhow, between my black curly hair and my white handkerchiefs, they wanted me to be a salesman. I picked things up quickly, especially the French polishing they did: grounding, spraying, painting; touching up dented items by hand.

But I'd only gone in by mistake! I thought it was involved with textiles, but it wasn't – Dad and I were mistaken, signing me up for a job that had nothing to *do* with textiles. I did the *wrong job* for two months. Which is fine: you can learn something from any job, for a while.

After two months I left for the Calico Printers Association, a textile factory, and within the first six months there, I'd found what you might call my true talent.

My career as a male model

Surprising no one, in 1949 or 1950 I was made a model for the Lancashire textile industry's advertising campaign. One has to keep busy. In the photos, I held some *kangas* – rough-feeling South African garments. They took a photograph of me holding a roll of the fabric and put me in the brochures and posters. It was the first modeling I'd done.

Later on, when I was on the *Countess*, they photographed me with a couple of models for one of the marketing brochures. Another day at sea serving drinks to beautiful women and banking a decent wage. As they say here in America, 'No big deal.'

Then, when I lived in Puerto Rico with Cata, we'd just come back from New York I believe, and Cata's brother lent me a sports shirt, blue with a white stripe on the shoulder. *Quite* ugly. I didn't have a collection back then, beyond a few suits. I went to the supermarket, and Proctor & Gamble were doing a survey of some sort, which I took. I didn't realize what it was for until I got home that night, and saw myself on the news. *Bleeding hell,* I thought, *That's me, wearing the worst shirt in all of America.*

That's the full extent, thus far, of my modeling career: two hits and a miss, so to speak.

I think of the bullet that missed my head on the train to Wigan, of pouring drinks for those two models on the Cunard *Countess*, and of escaping the man with a knife at my farewell party in Kure. *Lucky*, I tell you – even if I did have to sneak out of the party barefoot...

At any rate: to anyone who's ever said I had a face for radio, I say *Piss off*, and thank you very much.

CHAPTER 7

Korea, Japan

I joined the British Army in 1952 as part of National Service; we all had to put in two years. I registered on the 1st of July, and left for Korea on the 9th of April, 1953. You had to be 19 to go to Korea, and the 9th was the day after my birthday – so they didn't leave much chance of me checking out, did they.

They send me to Japan, to the midget submarine base at Kure, where I spent the rest of the war.

I was demobbed on the last day of June 1954 after my two years were up. Some people would have been glad to get out even an *hour* early, but they had it harder than I did. Again, I was lucky – I enjoyed every minute of my time in Japan. It was like my home from home.

And the only people I had to fight were British.

I should tell you that what follows is *not* a tale of wartime heroism, except for the bit with the dancer.

It started poorly.

The day that I registered for the army, I had to go for a medical at an office across the road from Strangeways prison – well known in those days. They hanged a lot of people there, though I scraped by with just the medical.

Now, the man doing the eye test, he asked me, —What's the situation with your eyes?

I'd been working in textiles, and my vision had started to blur somewhat. —The stripes seem to intermix a bit.

—Well, this first test you shouldn't find difficult, anyhow. Next to the window you'll see a sign with some letters, and they're exceptionally large. I'm sure you can read them out for me.

There was an advert for Bisto on the wall of the prison – the gravy browning. No points for guessing what happened next.

—B-I-S-T-O, I said.

—Oh, we have a comedian here.

I wasn't being funny, though. He's just said 'exceptionally large.'

They still made me join the army though.

Let's get this out of the way early as well: I went AWOL from the reinforcement camp at Bicester with Denny Hagen from Manchester.

You had to draw tickets out of a hat to go on vacation at Easter, and Denny and I were two of the lucky ones – we both got to go on leave. Denny's girlfriend was coming to London with her cousin, which was ideal for both of us. We would stay with them for the weekend, then come back. Arrangements were made, as they say.

Denny was in love with her; I don't know if they got married – we never saw each other after the war.

Now, the sergeant was a Londoner. And for *some* reason, he said, —Oh, there's been a mistake. We'll have to do the draw again.

He might as well have said, —Oh, the *northerners* aren't going on leave, we'll make sure the London lads do.

He was what we call 'swinging it on us.' Doing a dirty trick, taking advantage. And of course the next draw didn't go our way

– Denny and I had to be on guard duty, holding a rifle and walking up and down across the bleeding highway.

Denny told me straight, —I'm going AWOL.

Now, AWOL – 'Absent Without Official Leave' – is a serious offence. You could be five years in prison for that. Plus I'd have been stuck with the work. —Denny, you can't leave me here crossing the road all day with a rifle, all on my own. You can't do that.

—Wally, come with me.

—For the sake of a girl?

—I'm going. (He knew they'd done a dirty trick on us, and as I say, he was in love.)

What could I do? I wasn't going to stay there and look a bleeding idiot walking around all day; it's not as if the Koreans were going to invade Bicester. —Besides that, they're more likely to notice one guy parading than no one there at all.

People in business call this 'strategic thinking.'

Well, we went. Two beautiful girls, great, and we went to the pub. They had a piano playing, and when we walked in the woman who ran the place said, —We've got two of the lads here from the army. Going to Korea, are you? Come on then, let's have a collection for the lads...

They passed a hat around for us. We only got a pound a week wages; she collected four pounds from the people at the pub. — Here you are lads, this is for you...and half for me, of course.

She kept two pounds. That's the fighting spirit!

All the same, two pounds paid for the night out with the girls, so we were quite happy. And one thing led to another, and we went back to camp. I was worried about what was coming, quite serious about it. —Denny, let's go back a little bit early, and face the trouble before the lads get in, so we won't be over embarrassed.

We arrived at 7:00 in the morning. There was nobody on the gate, meaning we had not yet been replaced, which was good news at least. We'd put the rifles under the leaves in the woods, perhaps 25 yards from the gate, so we went and got them – still in our uniforms, mind you – and started pacing the gates. Just after seven, the first truck drove up and started unloading, and we kept crossing the road with our rifles. The officers arrived. No one said anything to us.

We kept up until lunchtime.

The officer came out: —C'mon, you're relieved of duty, you lads, get yourselves a good meal.

We did so. At this point, I was starting to think we might make it.

After a bit, the officer came into the barracks, where we were sitting with the lads who'd come back from leave. He said, — Who were the lads who were on duty this weekend?

—Dutch and Denny, they told him.

—I've got some news for you if you want.

As they say in detective stories, 'the jig was up.' The officer turned to us and told us our fate:

—They're doing a movie down the road with Alan Ladd, and if you want to participate, they'll pay you expenses, cigarettes, alcohol, whatever. And food for two days of course.

Denny Hagen looked the officer in the eye and said, —Well, we deserve it, after being on duty *all bleeding weekend.*

So the next thing is, we go meet Alan Ladd.

The movie was about the paratroop division during the Second World War. In America they call it *Paratrooper;* in England it was called *The Red Beret.* You've got Donald Houston, Leo Genn, and Thomas Heathcoat. Anton Diffring was in it as well. And of course Alan Ladd in the lead – a beautiful man, golden haired, with beautiful hands. The lads wanted his autograph, so I volunteered to go in and interview him about it.

They wouldn't allow Ladd to do the jumps, because he'd injured his ankle – insurance and so forth. I went up to the mobile home where he was staying, and we talked a bit. I was good mannered and so forth, but he seemed quite down. I think he was in love with someone or other at the time, but I didn't know that. I tried to buck him up: —The lads are saying what a wonderful actor you are, you're handsome, you've got the world at your feet...

He'd done *Shane* by then, of course. *The Red Beret* wasn't any great movie from his perspective, of course, but as far as I was concerned, he was on top of the world.

I was an 'extra,' playing a soldier. In one scene, the officer tells us we've been given the wrong uniforms, and would be invading North Africa instead of some other place. I was sat right behind Alan Ladd – and that was my grand film debut. You can see me in the video, though honestly you may have to squint a bit; look for the black curly hair.

Now, this is a true story. I'd got involved with a chap called Schultz. There weren't many Jewish lads in the army, so I suppose he was the one. And we'd talk, and joke around. So I ran into him one day. He was going on vacation. I asked him, — Do you want to buy a suit?

—How much?

—Five pounds.

—It's a good suit, he said. —Can I pay you when I come back?

—You're joking, aren't you. I did want the money though, so I asked, —Where the hell are you going?

—I'm on leave for three days. I can't give it you until next week. I don't carry money with me.

Now, Schultz wasn't that big, so I figured if he didn't pay me, I could give him a good hiding. So I let him have the suit.

A few days later he comes back from vacation. —Here's your five pounds.

—Great! Glad you felt it was worth it. Did you have to dig under a tree or into your biscuit tin to get your five pounds?

—Oh no, he said. —I sold it for eight...

—What?

—...on the *train.*

—Bleeding hell.

Did I tell you I only went to school for four years? But I got an education all the same.

I hit a sergeant once – slapped his face. I think we were in Egypt.

Well, you need to keep busy somehow.

There were eight of us in the Ordnance Corps on the transport ship headed east – one of them was Frankie Croker the thief, if I remember right, and a chap named Lubbock, the only other private out of the 15th-19th battalions. Lubbock and I had volunteered to go to Korea—

I should explain something. My son points out that *volunteering* to go to Korea was arguably a bit foolish, as there was a war on.

Well, I didn't like the food in England, where I was stationed. It was bravado – I may have been intoxicated, I'm not sure. It certainly wasn't bravery.

In the camp where I was, Blackdown in Bicester, we were sat down at our meal, and they called us outside. But I was enjoying the food... —Just give me a minute, sergeant! I said. —I'm a slow eater.

In strategic terms, as they say, this was 'a terrible mistake.' They put me on seven days CB: Confined to Barracks.

Which reminds me of an old joke: a young private moved from one camp to another, and asked how the food was. — Bleeding terrible, they said, —but don't complain. The chef's brother is commanding officer.

So he goes in for a meal at the canteen, and the commanding officer comes around. He's had his meal, and it's crap of course. The command officer asks, —How do you find the food?

He says, —It's shit! But it's *well cooked*.

As my son would say, 'It's all in the delivery...'

Anyhow, the food at Blackdown was a bit rough. —I'm a slow eater, sergeant!

—Well, you're not here for a holiday.

He put me on a charge. Off to a good start.

There was a chap called Titchy Byrne in our unit who was just a bit taller than a dwarf. He wanted to go to the White Hart in Oxford, which wasn't far from where we were stationed at the time. I think we were getting ready to leave for Korea.

Now, Titchy liked to *fight*. It was a bit of fun for him. So the next thing is, we've gone in this pub, a fight started. And he ran right into it. I didn't want anything to do with it, did I. But somebody hit me, give me a right crack. I went to punch them and missed completely. Somebody else grabbed my neck, dragged me out of the pub, and they've got Titchy as well. It's the MPs, of course. They marched us to the police station, then back to camp.

We were put in the brig overnight. The following day I was asked about the situation. I said, —I went to hit somebody because they'd hit me, but I missed. I've never actually *hit* anybody. And on top of that, my colleague – he's braver than me – he was enjoying himself. But you can put me down as a Frankie Howard – a coward.

The officer understood. So they gave me seven days CB (Confined to Barracks), and Titchy Byrne got twenty-one.

Other than that, I wasn't involved with Titchy, which was lucky for me, I imagine. I might have ended up in a wee bit of trouble, if you'll pardon the expression.

I should say: *more* trouble.

Now I'm onboard ship, headed to Korea, and we've arrived in port. We'd been waiting awhile, and the lads were getting restless; there was a war on, after all. There was an engineer, a sergeant, who came across to where we were sitting, and I decided to have a word with him. For the common good and all.

—Now what's going on, Sarge? The Black Watch have gone ashore, the King's Own are going ashore now. What about us?

He said to me, a bit nasty, —What about you? You wait here. *I'll* tell you when to go.

I don't know if you've aware of this, but the Engineers were what you might call...well, I want to put this diplomatically: they were the lowest form of humanity in uniform. They clean the toilets. No respect, no glory. We were the Ordnance Corps – supplies, and even that counts as a step up. I felt, and I think we all felt, he was misusing his position.

So I slapped his face. —And you're lucky I'm not punching the bollocks off you.

He called the police and put me in the brig. You know what it is to slap a sergeant: 'Insubordination.'

But that wasn't the worst of it. When you're put in the brig ashore, behind bars but in a building, it's nothing compared with being in the bottom of a ship going back...and forth...and back...and forth, one side and another.

We had four weeks to go. Egypt, Israel, Ceylon, India, Kowloon, Singapore... Not in that order, I expect.

They came down to the brig for me about 10:30 at night. The trial was to take place just outside the room where I'd been held.

I couldn't even stand up. I was absolutely sick. Two MPs came in and lifted me up, carried me into the 'courtroom,' and held me up the entire time the trial took place.

A brigadier led the parade into the room. —What was the situation?

I said, quite bravely under the circumstances I think, —Sir, he's not Ordnance Corps, he's an *engineer* with a complex and some petty jealousy. I only *slapped* his face, by the way sir, though I wanted to punch him. He took a liberty with us lads, sir, and if there was trouble he looked for it – though if you feel that's trouble I completely disagree. To this day I would still like to give him a crack. He deserves one.

I think my face was as green as an apple.

The brigadier turned around and said to the other officers, — I think this man has suffered sufficiently, and see no reason why he should suffer anymore. Case dismissed.

Now that a few years have passed, I don't mind telling you: I think I got away with one there.

At any rate, we made it to Pusan in one piece and they didn't throw me out of the army on the way. But now came the real test: here we are in Korea, and the ack-ack guns are pounding across the water. I wasn't frightened, but I wasn't keen on going *toward* the guns. We'd been waiting for about 18 hours to disembark. The battalions had been assigned duties and gone off already: the Duke of Wellington's, the Black Watch, the King's Own. Lubbock and I were called into this room, and the colonel said, —You are to be sent to a midget submarine base in Japan, in a place called Kure.

He used a codeword for it, something ridiculous. I couldn't understand what the hell he was talking about. —You will be going *there*.

In other words, *away* from the guns.

It was the best thing that had happened to me in my life! Lubbock and me, we got to Kure, and at breakfast and lunchtime there were women waiting on us in the dining room, and the older women – *mamasans* – would make your bed, and keep the base clean.

And here I thought I'd volunteered for a *war!*

I've mentioned a few times, I know, that I pride myself on keeping neat and tidy. You might not think of that as a weakness, but life is funny that way.

I was an NCO, a Corporal, in charge of 31 people on my station, men and women, British and Japanese. If you needed a gun, clothing, any supplies, you came to us. Goods going to Korea and coming back passed through our base. I oversaw all that. Occasionally you'd get clothes coming back from Korea with personal things in the pockets – letters and such. It was a bit emotional; often these people had been injured, or passed on.

Anyhow, I was in a position to have what I wanted in terms of supplies. And that had created a problem.

You don't need to be on the front line for the war to touch your life, your emotions. Well, I'd already learned that as a child.

Prior to us getting there, there had been a bit of a mutiny in the unit. We'd have a Saturday Morning Inspection, 7am if I remember correctly, where the commanding officer would order a full inspection of the unit, meaning your bed is made and all your kit is on display: shoes and boots polished, clothes clean and folded. You had to be able to see your face in the boots.

I was always smart then, actually, but that was true before I went into the army. And afterward – I say that without ego. And I could get whatever I needed from my work. So I had a pair of officer's boots, brown, very beautiful. I dyed them black with ink, if I remember rightly, and lacquered the toe. The toe was beveled, and you'd take the bevel out with a bone (the back of your toothbrush, say). Laborious work, which you'd do quietly on your own. But whereas the men in the unit would have one pair of boots that might get scuffed or scarred, meaning they needed regular treatment, I had two pairs, including these officer's boots that I'd taken. They *glowed*.

I'd wear them to inspection. I remember one Saturday, I was standing in the center line of the squad, and the sergeant came in to inspect the unit. He said, —I want the first line to move forward four yards and the rear line to move backwards four yards. The center line to the right of Corporal Holland, turn right and move forward six yards, the same on the left.

They formed a square around me. The officer was making a big deal out of something – for his own purpose.

—You can all see the condition of Corporal Holland's boots, he said. —The work that he's put in is exemplary. I want *every man's boots* in that condition.

—Oh yes, we'll get them like that, they all said. They came closer to me, made a bit of a fuss. —How'd you manage to get them so shiny, Dutch? Just get ready to take them off when you get back to quarters so they don't get ruined.

We stayed in a long room, fifteen of us on each side. When we returned, I went to the bed, and all the lads came to my bed.

And one of them was holding a razor blade. —All right, take 'em off, Dutch.

I did. The lads came forward and picked up the boots, and proceeded to cut them to pieces with the razors.

They hung them up on the top of my locker. —*That's* how we want your boots to look, for the future.

Even I had to laugh. I didn't know it would cause that kind of problem for everyone else. I just wanted to look smart, stay tidy.

I don't think anyone's worn more different *uniforms* than me: football, army, the airline, the ship... I know it's a silly thing to say. But I think of how many countries I've been to. A lot of people have seen as many countries as me, but they can *afford* to travel, you see? I didn't get to Japan or India or South Africa because I had money and a few days with nothing to do. I *worked* at it – in the Army, in the airlines, on the ship. Everywhere I went, I showed up in one uniform or another, even if it was technically just a Bermuda shirt.

When my son went to the National Spelling Bee the first time, one of the local TV stations came and interviewed me. I think the management wanted a bit of 'star power.' A couple of years ago I was on the radio here in Western New York, with the Springville Arts Society – we did *It's a Wonderful Life* and *A Christmas Carol*. I was in a film with Alan Ladd, danced onstage in Japan with Ivor Novello's leading lady, acted with my eldest son in *On Golden Pond*, and later on I did plays by Agatha Christie, Neil Simon, Arthur Miller.

I think the French call it 'quite a *résumé*,' with a bit of a gurgle sound on the 'r.'

The dancing is technically a war story, by the way. I was on guard duty. The leading lady was giving a theatre appearance upstairs. I crept up to the end of front row, trying to keep from being seen. A dozen seats from me were the colonel, the adjutant. The leading lady asked for a young man to help with her next number. I'm sat down in the chair, my legs stretched out, my head as low as I can make it. I'm *certain* I did a good job hiding.

The adjutant turned around and said, —Corporal Holland, you're not supposed to be here, you're on duty. *You* get up there.

Well, I got onstage; you have to follow orders. She was a buxom woman, perhaps fifty years old, all in powder and rouge and perfumes. It was overwhelming: her hairstyle, her bright red lipstick.

We started singing a song. And she drew my head into her bosom, which I alluded to a moment ago. Many men have found themselves in this situation and panicked, but I've been around the block: without hesitating I wiggled my head around. — *Whooooaaaa!* Like that. She pushed me away, hit me across the face, and said, —None of that nonsense!

I couldn't stop laughing, and neither could she. She couldn't sing the song, she was laughing so hard. But a moment later, she got her breath, and we finished the song together.

We *brought the house down.* All the guys were calling out: — Well done, Dutch!

Even the officers couldn't stop laughing, which is lucky for me, as *strictly* speaking I had abandoned my post.

It was spontaneous. I get that way sometimes, joking around. It's my kind of humour. It was a bit low class, in a way, but at that moment it seemed the right thing to do.

The right thing isn't always the appropriate thing, as they say.

I mention this – the dancing, the film, radio, acting onstage – not to boast, but to marvel at it. How many people can say they've done all these things? I don't mean proper entertainers, but everyday people. How many kids, come from nothing, can say that? I feel proud about it.

For so many years, when people tell me stories about seeing something on television or reading a story in the paper, I often find myself saying: —Oh yes, I was there many years ago. Or: —Oh I've met him, actually.

In case that's a bit hard to believe, now I've set it down in writing.

Overall I'd say there are fewer bosoms in this memoir than there might have been.

'Always leave them wanting more,' as they say.

I should mention the Australian.

There were eight of us in our room in the barracks in Japan. Instead of a door there was a mesh over the doorframe, and the rooms were never locked. My bed was underneath the window, and twenty yards away was the adjutant.

With us there were the Australians, the Canadians, the Maoris – all stationed together, in different sections of the camp, happy to do a favour for the Queen. And this Australian...well, in addition to all the sake he'd been drinking, he'd caught syphilis, a very serious thing. I knew the Australian's name at the time; we all knew each other and were quite friendly. (You had no choice, really.) The Australians were in charge of the guns. Looking back, that seems like a mistake.

His girlfriend was an Australian nurse. She was coming over to be stationed in the local hospital, meaning she'd soon find out, if she didn't already know, that he'd gotten black syphilis – the important detail here is that he'd not gotten it from *her*. And of course, the moment she found out, she broke off the engagement. The adjutant seems to have been responsible for getting the information to the nurse.

So naturally the Australian wanted to shoot him.

You may recall where my bed was located: beneath the window. He knelt on me to reach it. He had a gun, and was trying to break the window with it. Naturally, I woke up. —I'll blow your f'ing head off, he said. I believed him.

As they say: I'm glad I was wearing brown underwear.

There was a Scottish corporal in the bed next to me – I mean the *next bed,* we weren't *that* close – who'd been in the army about eighteen years. He was quite old, a small fellow, and always looked completely knackered – a good meal would kill him. He wasn't the only one, of course; back then, you'd have people joining the army just to have a uniform to wear and a decent meal. Dad used to tell me so during the war, and he knew: he'd volunteered in 1916.

(Dad's army stories were a bit like mine, which was lucky for both us, I suppose.)

I can still remember the barracks quite clearly. We had lockers for our things in the center of the room. Four of them for eight people in the room, each with two uniforms.

Our uniforms were the *worst* in all the armed forces. Even the Australians had a nicer uniform than we did. We used to 'shave' them – the English uniform was very hairy, and would irritate bare skin. We had 'safari suits' in dark green, and you could have them starched, so the jacket would look tidy (without starch: absolutely terrible). I brought a couple of these jackets back to England when I returned – maybe I bought them in Africa? – and gave them to Dickie Rogers, my old pal from next door at Stonyhurst.

Back to the occasion under discussion. They put the Australian out straight away, put him on a charge, and sent him back to Australia. I assume his girlfriend stayed on.

Concerning certain colonial subjects

I knew a man who emigrated from Manchester to Australia. He was in his forties. You'd get guys like him, older, joining the army for a bit better life, as I spoke of before. The Australians would always greet you: —How are ya, blue? You alright, mate?

I've no idea where 'blue' came from. Australians, you see?

Americans used to ask me if *I* were Australian. My God! Your voice does change as you travel, but I still speak *English,* don't I?

When I was in with the Scottish regiment, the Black Watch, you'd hear a lot of this:

'...'[1]

...the Glasgow slang, you know. The worst language in the *world*, bar none, whereas in Edinburgh, where my father-in-law studied, they speak the most beautiful English one can hope to hear. In Glasgow, you might hear this: '...'[2] which translates to 'I shall not tell you again what I want you to do.'

Embarrassing, really.

I know this story goes from side to side a bit, but that's how it comes to you: each memory brings another with it, which might move you a day forward or forty years back. It's like pulling on a thread.

We were talking about Korea, weren't we.

---

[1] Imagine a string of unintelligible gibberish followed by *'I'll no' tell y'agin'*

[2] Same again, with more cursing.

There were some lads from Manchester with me in the army, like Denny Hagen whom I went AWOL with – he lived ten miles from me in Manchester, but I never saw him again after I left the army. If you wanted something more than what you had, you had to go looking for it, go your separate ways.

Bob Martin, who I met on the ship, was a local lad – I knew his brother from playing soccer, from the pubs. Within about a year of us coming back, he got married, in a suit he'd bought in Hong Kong.

You could always buy beautiful things in Hong Kong. Silk shirts, gabardine suits. Cigars, alcohol. (Sex, of course, which I won't go on about in case there are children reading.) They certainly looked forward to the ships coming in.

Now, with the education I'd had off my father and Unkie, I was always on my toes – quick to assess a situation. Guys trying to put one over on me, that sort of thing. I made my share of mistakes, don't get me wrong – I think of a particular 'gold' ring I bought; I think I was upset over that for fully four years. A *lot* of money, that was.

Going overseas, though, was a revelation. When we first arrived in Hong Kong, there was a dead body floating at the side of the ship...and it was of *no consequence* to anyone around. Later, a bomb had been put onboard the ship. On the way back, we had a lunatic who went overboard, a crosseyed fellow with a girlfriend back home. This fellow jumped right over the side of the ship. They pulled him out, of course. He had a girl in Japan, you see, probably the first he'd ever had in his life. So he wasn't eager to go home.

It turns out that for a lad from Manchester, the rest of the world is...a different world.

I remember an old lady from Liverpool, when the ship left England – she walked down the dock as we sailed away. 'God bless you,' she was shouting to us. 'We love you!' She'd had a couple of beers. 'Look after yourselves, we love you! God bless you!' It was quite emotional, actually.

Some of the lads never came back, you see.

Some who went there with me – in the Black Watch, the Green Howards – they were killed within a few months. It hardly seems fair: I left England the 9th of April, we took five weeks to travel there, and I believe the armistice was signed in July. My own stories about the war are more funny than sad, I hope, but it was a *war* after all. I didn't see combat, but I saw some of what it did.

Our submarine base in Kure was the first stop on the way home from Korea, so all the people who were prisoners of war or injured, they were all released in Japan on the way back.

Some of them would be put in the hospitals there, but some would be on their way home, and at leisure. The way I remember it, everybody wore a blue jacket and white trousers.

Now, when someone's been a captive for years, they're right full of beans – you've no idea what they're going to do next, and half the time *they* don't know either. The law in Japan was that you're guilty until you're found innocent, and you couldn't have that for soldiers. So no matter what the soldiers did – if they smashed a place up, there was no charge involved. Some of them were...well, completely mad. Berserk. The MPs would just go in and get them, put them back on the ship. Allowances had to be made for their mentality.

There's a joke about a guy who worked in a mental hospital, and he went to a large restaurant nearby and said, 'Look here. We've arranged a trip, and these people need to eat. Now, they're from the mental hospital. Any damage they do, I will pay you accordingly. Make sure they have a good meal – we've quite a journey to make – and I will pay for anything they do, perchance any damage is done.'

Well, the man in charge thought that was very kind. 'Of course! We're glad to have them in.'

And they had a marvelous meal. Everything on their plates. And then – they started breaking everything up, the glasses, the cups, everything!

The owner said to his staff, 'Stand back, let them do as they will. It's been seen to.'

So they clear everyone out at the end, back to the mental hospital. The guy comes back. 'How much is it I owe you now?' The head waiter tells him. The man nods. 'Alright – well, can you make change for this dustbin lid?'

Goodbye to all that

I had 31 staff under me at in Kure. When I was to be demobbed and sent back to England, they threw a large party in my honour. Maxie Carpenter and his wife were there. Maxie was a rugby player from Australia. To give you a sense of him: when we ran the 100 yards, he beat me. He was 43 years old at the time, and I was 19, so you can imagine...

Now, in Japan they give you special slippers to walk around inside the house, and put your shoes away. Naturally they did the same at this party for me. But there was a Japanese fellow whom I'd fired, who was apparently holding some sort of grudge against me. And at the party I was told that he was on the premises, and said to be carrying a knife.

It was reported by the staff that he was coming after me, since I'd fired him.

I didn't realize at the time that he was a submarine captain – a marvelous honour – and that in Japan, to reach that status and then be insulted by me, a young man and an invader in a way, was a dishonour. I could understand him being angry at me!

Still, I didn't want to see him right then.

They hustled me out of the house in quite a hurry. Maxie's wife went with me and drove me home in the jeep.

A few days later, I asked Maxie to see that the gentleman was given his job back, and I believe they did so. It's funny, in a way – I had grown up hating the Japanese, during the war, but in my time there I came to love their culture, to *respect* them – their dignity. We don't have that dignity anymore, I think.

That was one of the few really good things I've done in my life, getting that man his job back. There was another time years later: I did a good turn for a colleague at the airline, BEA, and it cost me dearly.

There's a decent side of me, and it's been there since I was young. I believe it's still there.

That's not why I told you the party story, though. Rather, I want to make a complaint: they hurried me out of the party and *left my bloody shoes behind.*

Demobbed

This isn't quite a Korea story, though I do almost get stabbed. *Again.*

When I got back to London from Japan, I went to Soho – a bad part of the city, with more gangsters than you might consider healthy. I was with a chap from the NAAFI – 45, 46 years of age, very small. (The 'naffy' is the people that look after supplies, the cantina.) There I am, 20 years of age, with a decent suntan, black curly hair. And these two beautiful women stroll by, both in their 30s. The older one was married – she said she'd just become a prostitute for the first time, which I was happy to believe. The other was an exceptionally *experienced* blonde in her 40s. They had nice two-piece costumes, nice legs...

We'd been away from home for years. They were enticing, so to speak.

Now, we're on Brewer Street, in the part of town dominated by Jack Spot, a very famous criminal. This was a very shady part of London, where you had to be on your toes.

Anyhow, we headed back to the building where these women lived and worked. The woman I was with had two kids. She was very nice to talk to. The other fellow was in the next room with the blonde woman. As I say, she was more experienced – she'd seen the roll of the coin, so to speak. But now I hear a scream from the other room. So I head over there.

Well, he didn't want to pay her for some reason, and he was angry about it – he was starting to get violent with her. So I had to get him off of the poor woman. I yell at him, —Come on, we're getting out of here.

We come out of the rooms to the top of the stair. And there's two men standing there, one 6'4" if he's an inch, another normal height – but the smaller one has a shiv in his hand, which had my attention.

—So you want to start some trouble, do you?

The man I was with was pissed out of his head. But he was 40-odd years old – even sober he couldn't have done anything about these two. And now they're starting to threaten us: *I'll kick your f'ing head in,* and all that. Things weren't going all that well.

So I turned to the fellow from the naffy and hit him, as best I could. He went down, and I turned to the two fellows and their shiv. —Just let us out, lads, I said.

I had to speak the way they did, you see: —This *f'ing so-and-so,* give us a chance to get out of this *bleeding building,* and so forth.

—Alright, son.

I was genuinely grateful, believe me, as I started carrying him down the stairs. —Not looking for trouble by any means, let me get this *f'ing lunatic* out of here, you know how it is. (Laying it on a bit thick.)

Not my usual way of speaking, but I knew how to handle myself.

The last fight I got into onboard ship, later in life, there were five of them wanting to fight me, and the smaller one said something to me. The other four I couldn't have beaten – so I smacked the smallest one instead. He went down quickly and I was on top of him – I might've killed him, honestly – but I came to, and let him go. I started crying. I'd had a dirty trick done on me, I didn't like it, but I thought, *I'm not going to take it out on this man.*

I've not fought anyone since, come to think of it.

I did have a temper when I was younger. Not anymore, not the same. Mind you, with this pacemaker I shouldn't be fighting anyway – if someone hit me I'd spin around like a corkscrew.

You know, I must have gotten those shoes back from the farewell party at some point, since I didn't have to go barefoot on the ship back from Japan. But I can't remember. Still, if you forced me to choose, I'd rather have the story than the shoes.

CHAPTER 8

A trade

When I got back from Korea, I wasn't ready to go back into textiles – I didn't want to be cooped up inside. I hadn't seen combat, as they say, but I had seen what happens to boys who have to fight. And I'd been handling dead men's effects on the base in Kure. It changes you, in a way.

After two years, I wanted to be out in the open.

After St Augustine's was destroyed by the land mine during the war, I'd been friends with a lad named Brian Lillis. He was a big lad, quite tubby actually (a lot less common in those days), younger than us. When I got back to England from Japan, I joined a football team, Lloyds Celtic. Brian was the captain, and most of the characters on that team had been in school together as well. We were a smashing team – unbeaten in 31 games.

Brian was working in asphalt. He had a contract, meaning he'd need himself and another man as spreaders – the ones who do hand-work on the floor, the main job; a potman, who'd look after the pot and keep it all hot; and the labourer. When I came out of the army, as I say, I'd been an apprentice for seven years in textile designs, and needed something new for a while. So I worked with Brian on the asphalt as a labourer instead.

Working with asphalt, one of the things you'd do was to piss on your hands, to toughen the skin. Workers would do the same thing in Africa, as I understood it: stand in the urine to toughen their feet.

I imagine you think that's horrible. Mind you, we used to brush our teeth with soot and salt, during rationing. So we were used to another way of life.

And I was outside, which was the most important thing. Not cooped up.

(If you *don't* think the bit about pissing on your hands and feet is horrible, that's all right, but for God's sake *don't tell anybody*.)

It's not that the wages were good, working with Brian, but you ended up making good money, because you got a bonus for finishing quickly – which we always made, every job – plus expenses. The better you were at the job, the better you did for yourself, and we were pretty good.

Now, Brian and I had something else in common, besides the football club: he used to bet on the horses as well.

This becomes relevant in a moment.

On one occasion, we'd gone to Liverpool. It was a pull-up job on Lime St, which meant we were working on the roof, which I'd say was about 18-20 foot high. Now, when you're working on asphalt, you're carrying two 56-pound buckets up to the roof, one in each hand – 112 pounds altogether – then you'd tip it carefully. There was a knack you had to acquire, to make it smooth and even.

With a pull-up job, one bucket at a time was no problem. But when the job was complete, there'd be quite a lot of pieces and bits to pick up, – something that hadn't been boiled enough, wasn't hot enough, you'd toss it on the side, so that when you'd leveled the roof off, you could gather the bits and pieces and they'd go back in the boiler.

We'd been working for a few days, and we'd finished the job. Everything was packed up. Instead of the empty bucket – and the buckets themselves were made of steel, very heavy – when the job was finished, all the extra bits were put into the buckets. And then, being on the end of the rope downstairs, the buckets would be lowered down to me. Now remember, twice 56 is 112 pounds going up and down. Now, in the aftermath of the job, there was more than 112 pounds in it. There were two buckets filled with rubbish. They called down, —Right, Wally!

They dropped the bucket down on the pulley. The bucket came down and I went up.

Eighteen feet.

I laugh *now*, but I had eighteen blisters. They had to go up and get me out of the air. My hands were bad, but they allowed me to work after that, to get paid. Which I was entitled to, I suppose.

What did the Superman movie used to say? 'You'll believe a man can fly.'

Well, the next thing Brian says to me is, —We're having a dollar bet today. (A dollar was five shillings.)

I said I didn't have a dollar on me. —Can you leave it 'til Saturday when you pay me?

Brian said, —You can have half of what I put on.

And of course, the three horses won. He'd put all the money on, now he had to give me half. —Bleeding hell, he said, —This is *mine*.

—Brian, you're *employing* me. You don't want me to...accidentally...say that I left this person's employ because he was a bleeding dishonest miser.

He told me to piss off, and I got half the winnings. He gave it to me gladly, *after* saying no. I was flying – which made it twice that day I'd been up in the air.

And do you know: one of the horses was called 'Blisters.'

Another job: working for two twins, the Vospers, who were making a lot of money. There was another chap called Walter. He borrowed £5 off me (I'd made a bit of money at the time), which he never paid back, by the way. I never saw him again. Walter, if you're reading this, you swine, send me the money care of the Ellicottville Library, where I read my email.)

The Vospers were doing a particular job; we finished the contract pretty quickly and they said, —Do you want to go home?

I said, —Not particularly, no.

—Well, we'll have to contract you out to the road gang, Wally.

—What's the road gang doing, I asked.

—The roads.

The foreman on that job didn't like me. He thought I was of the noble rich, because I'd wear a white shirt or whatever. Petty jealousy: you get that in life. He said to me, —I want you to do this job: sweeping the roads.

I said, —Who normally does it?

He pointed to another chap: —Him. But we want to put him on this other thing.

I said, —I'll tell you what. Put *me* on there and put him doing the roads.

—Oh no, he said. —The road's for you. It won't do you any harm.

—It won't do me any good either.

And then, as I had enough money saved up to get by for a few weeks, I told him where he could stick the job, using what my son calls 'vivid language.'

Which is how I left the asphalt business.

Working with Brian, I was one of the crowd; but sometimes, when you've got power in the wrong hands, you see the other side of people. Some people shouldn't be in a position of authority.

Here's a story for you.

We'd taken a day trip to Redcar, Yorkshire, for the horses. It was Les Hicks, myself, and another chap. I'd been lucky on the first race, backed a winner each way.

Now, in those days Cassius Clay was a big name in England. He would do these wonderful monologues, speeches for reporters, and he had a way of rhyming words as he spoke... Anyhow, the name 'Morning Bloom' caught my eye. For some reason the name had that same music. I backed the horse and won at 14-1. The others on the trip didn't back it, just me – we wouldn't discuss that. Now, in Redcar, we're situated near Tattersalls Stalls, where the horses are held before and after the races. And after the race, I followed Morning Bloom to where the owner was. It was a woman in tweeds, oddly enough. I said,

—Excuse me ma'am, is this your horse?

—Well, I just want to you to know that *Morning Bloom lifts the gloom!*

—Yes, she said. There wasn't anything else to say!

I backed another winner later that day, but for some reason that horse had given me a special feeling. I was over the moon, you know. It was one of those days where you couldn't go wrong.

On the train back from the track, there were raffles on the coach. Now, there's no use lying at my age, and anyhow I don't tell lies, so you can believe this: there were six raffles and three of us, and we won *all six* between us. I forget what they were – boxes of chocolate, food, cake, cigarettes, and some money –

but we took them all. Each of us kept what he'd won for himself. It wasn't a case of sharing; we were friends, certainly, but...

Some days are like that, aren't they? And you can look back on them for the rest of your life and relive those feelings a little bit. They never quite leave you.

Les Hicks, the same chap that I went to the track with, he had a central heating business, laying the old-fashioned pipes and stoves along the walls. He asked me to work for him, and paid me very good money – he was a master plumber and builder. Steel. An intelligent lad.

Les asked me to work with him when I was with Brian. I said yeah; it'd be a better job than the asphalt, pay me more money and so forth. So I left the asphalt behind and worked with him for a while.

We were working on a job for a Jewish organization. I was Les's main man, handling the machine that needed to be spun around and so forth, a locking device – he showed me how to do all that. That's why he paid me a lot more money.

Anyhow, when we'd gone inside, this young man was in the corner of the room bowing his head against the wall; he had ringlets in his hair. I believe it's a special form of worship. He was praying. I didn't know that at the time! Well, with me only going to school for one minute, I was in the corner quite a bit myself: *Holland, get in the corner and wait!* and that sort of thing. So when I saw this guy, I said: —What have *you* done to deserve this?!

Of course, he never answered me.

The fellow with me said (quietly), —Wally, come *here*. That's part of their religion. He's praying.

I'd seen praying, of course; during games at Old Trafford, people call out for the Lord's assistance quite regularly. But I'd never seen *that* before.

Les occasionally knocked about with us, like the day at the track; mind you, he was married, so he didn't have as much time to fool around as some of us did. A very good soccer player – better than I was; he'd had trials for United. And a principled man, a *good* man: When I worked for him, he was offered an enormous contract, one of the biggest in England. But he turned it down, not because he didn't need the money, but because he didn't have the staff to do it properly.

In one of the houses we worked on, the cellar had been abandoned for a year or so. We found quite a lot of *copper* in the basement, very expensive – it was worth about £27, which was double my wages. It was me who found it, and Les looked after me accordingly – though he could easily have kept the money for himself.

Later on Les had four children, and a few years later, he was mowing his lawn and hit an electrical cord; it killed him. The children were quite young. Six months later, his wife was crossing the road to go to a party and she was run over by a motorbike.

They had been great friends of mine, once, and then they were gone; I remember them, and for a moment they're here again – but only for a moment.

I worked for a while at a firm with a fellow named Malcolm Tierney – you might have seen him murdering people in the movie *Braveheart*. You had a feeling Malcolm was going somewhere. He invited me to the pub one evening. I asked, — Why do you want to go with *me*, Malcolm, to Parkers, the best bar in town? He said, —Because my friends go there!

—Who the bloody hell are your friends?

—Well, I work for RADA – the Royal Academy of Dramatic Art.

—Never heard of it.

—Laurence Olivier's the top man there, Wally.

—Oh, him. Well, who are these friends of yours?

—Albert Finney and Tom Courtenay.

(I don't suppose you've heard of *them*, have you.)

Eventually I was offered a job with a leading textile company, Tootal Broadhurst & Lee. Perhaps they'd seen my modeling photos.

By then I'd qualified as a full-fledged pattern card maker. I might get four different fabric pieces, design the book, cut the material, and cut out cartilage to make the inside of the book, which would then be cut on a guillotine and pasted together with gum or glue. This wasn't as good as the old style of stitching, but it was faster, and cost less. That's what they call 'progress,' I think.

I'd also do embossing and decoration for the pattern books. I'd press a pattern into the cover, spray gold dust onto it, then move what they called a 'rabbit's paw' so that all the dust would go into where the impression had been made. I created patterns and advertising for the new necktie designs, and for what you might call 'shirtings' – shirts and cravats.

Having worked at these two or three textile firms, I was quite professional in my job; I knew what I was doing. After more than six years at Calico Printers, I'd had my apprenticeship, you might say. The work was enjoyable enough, and I enjoyed being quite good at it.

Much more importantly, there were a *lot* of beautiful girls there. You know, one of the girls at Tootal's won on the Pools,

£31,000 – which was like a million dollars today, in a way. A lot of money when your wages were £15 a week...

We had four adults and four young boys, apprentices. There was my best pal, David McMurdo, myself, and an Irish chap called Frank Mallone whose father was a big salesman for the food industry. He came a few months after David and myself. There was another Frank as well; I can't remember his second name.

(Years later, in Cornwall, one of the young ladies – there were several in those days – she was from the same part of Manchester as myself, and came to work at the hotel where I worked. We had an affair, with one thing and the other. But years later, she married that same Frank Mallone. Small world...

No: not so small, really. But we wouldn't have known if we hadn't gone and seen it for ourselves.)

I loved working at Tootal. I was very happy. I've done shit jobs over the years: cutting down Christmas trees, lifting patients in the nursing home. In the army, when they put you on CB, you might have to scrape toilet bowls with a razor blade, parade with a rifle with nobody watching – ours was a 'transition' camp, where you might have 1,000 men one day and 5,000 the next, so nobody knew who was who, which is how I managed to get away with going AWOL.

This was better than that.

In the textile factory, all these women, young and old, surrounded me at these long tables. They'd have to pass my table to go to the bathroom. We'd say hi, wave, nod... In normal life, at that age, to see a pretty girl seemed like a revelation. But I got to see them every day! And you have to give it your best shot: make sure you had a decent haircut, well combed, and try to look nice.

Working in textiles gave us some advantage there: in those days, Tootal would have special sales on excess fabric for the employees. A floor below us was the main distributor of the material that we used at the company. A sharply dressed man in his forties, divorced I think, and a real woman-chaser. He had to be with someone no matter who she was, what she looked like; since he had access to the fabric, he had an opportunity to pass on a length of material to a girl if she wanted a new dress. When Dave and I wanted anything, we had to deal with him – if we asked for a tie, we didn't get the tie itself, we'd get the *material*. So we had the ties made the way we wanted. Those were the perks. The ties wouldn't have gone to stores yet – and he'd give to Dave McMurdo and me a tie each (never to one without the other, mind you), because he loved talking to us about all the women at the factory. And they were always coming around.

Was his name 'Harry'?

Well: Harry would come up to the table, and with him being there, the girls would make sure to pass by our table on their way. And they wouldn't just say 'Hi Wally': I was in my twenties and had black curly hair, so they'd say, —*Hiiiii Wallyyyyyy...*

I loved it, me.

You'd pass the girls in the hallway, going to the bathroom, and they'd smile at you, which made your day. Of course, if they smiled *repeatedly*, and wanted to *talk*, you knew they wanted to be put on your list. But then you had to make a decision: *Do they deserve me, or not?* No two ways about it. Then you had to weigh up the pros and cons: how much will this *cost*, and so forth.

I saw *South Pacific* in the theatre with one of the girls from work, a blonde girl named Helen Bruce, and I offered to see her home. I'll always remember that she lived *miles* away, over where Georgie Best bought a house. Out in the country, in

Cheshire! So her family had a few bob, obviously. But I had to take her home! We took a bus, and I'd just hope that I could catch the last bus home. Otherwise I'd be stuck out there in heaven. *Miles* away from anything.

I made a vow that very day, after taking Helen home, that I'd never again get a girl that lived that far from the center of Manchester. I thought the bloody bus would *never* come.

Dave got that attention for a while, —*Hiii Dave...* and all that, but by then Dave was *engaged*. His fiancée Pat was too nice for me. I don't mean in terms of appearance, though she was very pretty, but rather her wonderful disposition. Where I loved a laugh and whatnot, I was more...well, mad, put it that way. Manically depressed or something. David was very steady. A good-looking guy, smart, smarter than myself – *just* smarter, mind you – and he'd ignore all the flirting and chattering, quite rightly so.

Dave was very much like me, to look at. The same build. We were competitive, as a matter of fact – any neckties we did at Calico Printers, we had some done up for ourselves. David had followed me from Calico Printers to Tootal and worked with me – and he was a better pattern card maker than myself. A more efficient person.

I want to stress, though, that Dave McMurdo was not perfect. I remember at least one *grave* mistake he made:

I went to Guernsey with Billy Moore. Now, I didn't have any money to go on this trip – it was £35 to go – so Billy Moore said, —I'll lend you the money.

I said, —£35? How the hell am I supposed to pay you that back?

I suppose it's typical for an older person to feel he has to say this, but for the benefit of any younger readers: '*That was a lot of money, then.*'

—I've already booked a ticket for you, he said.

I asked if he didn't want to give it me as a present...?

—Bleeding *hell*, he said.

Now, Mooresy, he knew that it was to his advantage to have me there on the trip. As regards the girls, and the laughs.

So he says, —You're going, aren't you Wally?

It's nice to be needed. I paid him.

So we went to Guernsey, as you do, and came back. And we'd used oil and dark vinegar to get a suntan. I am not exaggerating or making this up: I was taken for an Indian – that's how black I was from the sun.

Now, Dave always wanted to go somewhere different, which I admire about him, so he's gone to Czechoslovakia, and *he's* come back with a superb tan as well.

Prague: beautiful city. Not 'tropical' in the usual sense.

Now, the serrated-edge machines in Tootal were a few feet high, and longer than a full-grown man. You'd feed the fabric and the bookmaking material. The windows face the canal, and you'd move between your bench (facing the room) and the machine (facing the windows). My first day back at work, I walk onto the floor at Tootal's, and there's the back of David's head, across the room, his neck a deep brown. *Very* impressive suntan! And as I examine it more closely, a bit envious maybe, I see the strangest thing: the backs of his ears are white. Not 'less brown,' I mean white as a sheet.

Dave McMurdo had painted his body brown.

—What's that, Dave? You working on your Al Jolson impression?

He turned around, genuinely mortified. He'd been found out. —I had no *idea,* Wally. The sun *does not shine at all* in Czechoslovakia...

Dave was a fullback on a football team I played for, Melford Celtic. In my generation, defensive players never had much intelligence, or at any rate weren't accepted as having any. Dave had real intelligence like Roger Byrne or Johnny Carey, both of whom I saw play for United: he didn't just bang the ball downfield, he could give a square ball to me at wing-half, could use his head...

(Which reminds me of a story:

In 1953 I went to see Chelsea play – I think it was Tottenham. Chelsea won 1-0. The goalkeeper was Bonetti, an Italian. They had a great center-forward – good-looking lad, 6'2", similar to Tommy Taylor who played for England and United – and a chap called Frank Blunstone on the left wing. That weekend I went with Frankie Croker, the thief. I paid for him to come to the movies with me, as he had no money. And – have you ever seen a '3-D' film? When they throw something at you, you duck. (We had no idea.) I don't know if they do the same thing now, but they used to give you a pair of glasses.

We go in and the first thing Croker says to me is: —Hey, *these* must be worth a few bob, Wally.

'Ladies and gentlemen,' as they say, 'Frankie Croker.'

And now back to more respectable topics.)

If Dave was ever talking about me he'd say —Ohh, *he's* the best... Because I could play anywhere. (Well, except goalkeeper.) He always sang my praises. And yet we were the most competitive... Even the haircuts. He had good hair, as I did in those days.

Dave's younger brother got trials for United. They signed him on, and he played at a low level for them, but made a big mistake in his personal life. I never did know what it was, but he had to leave United. He was a smashing player. His brother was so upset, afterward. But Dave might have been the stronger player, all the same, if things had gone differently.

Dave was in the army like myself, and fell six feet down into a tank pit. He busted his knee, and they replaced it completely with a metal plate, which restricted him somewhat. At any rate, Dave's priority was always his girlfriend, whom he got engaged to. He never looked at another woman. (She was *beautiful*, which helped him focus.) And he stopped playing early because he wanted to make a bit more money, for the two of them. He went into business for himself, and he succeeded. As I knew he would – he was a clever boy.

I was traveling the world by then. I'd come home and Dave would say, —Are you ever thinking of settling down? (Out of all of us, I left it late, you see.) But I still wanted to go gallivanting. I wasn't ready yet.

Everything David wanted to do, he did – he wanted a house, he got a small one at a good price, decorated. They got the chance at a new home in the flamboyant district outside of Oldham. A proper domestic life, with a garden. The neighbours all said '*Ohhhh,*' that sort of thing. That was how David was: he wanted to progress, to climb the ladder. And he did: exactly what he wanted to do.

My father was a floor-layer, a designer, but in later years when there wasn't work, he took a job at the same factory as David's father, and they got to know each other. That made me so happy.

I could never respect a man more, or have had more laughs or a better friendship, than I had with David McMurdo. He laid out a map for himself in life – a wife, children, a good career – and he followed it. A wonderful man.

After coming back from Korea I lived with Dad again in Bark Street. This time I was able to provide a bit for the two of us, as I wasn't an apprentice anymore.

I remember I was working on a European design, two items that finished first and second in a competition. And the items were made of *fiberglass*, of all things. (It was still relatively new, then; I imagine for young people it's impossible to imagine *fiberglass* ever being new. But like everything else, once upon a time, it was.) The girls were handling small sections of it after we'd cut sets from the material, and we'd all get horrible rashes on their skin.

There were two patterns: bronze and light and dark greens on a silver background, and a mosaic design on a silver background, black and primrose. These were top designs at the time.

I cut hundreds of yards of the stuff, and I was able to save enough of that material to put in the house the government had provided for my father, 141 Darley Ave, Chorlton-cum-Hardy. I'd decorated and furnished it. I used the material for curtains, as they let the light in, almost like mosquito netting (mosquitoes not included).

I don't suppose it matters all that much to you, what the curtains looked like in my dad's house, what our street address was. But this is the way it comes to me: not in a straight line, but in pieces here and there. I think of the light through the curtains, the house next door, the cemetery across the road, the day Mum died. The kids stealing the fruit from our yard were me in another time. And in a way that's what my story is, now. So I tell the story in circles, so to speak, and when I've told it, there it is, and there I am.

In Oxford St in Manchester – you have the same street names in Manchester as in London, of course, Oxford and Piccadilly – there was a furniture maker. I chose this orange sofa, something modern, curved, and two chairs. Expensive, by the way. Another design winner. I bought them for Dad with my pension money I'd saved up, to go with the new fireplaces that were coming in, all tiles, with a mantel above. (Later on it would be charcoal walls and *orange ceilings* – we never had any of that in our house.)

Dad's house had electric lights and a bath, and the nicest garden on the row – the chap who'd been there before and passed away was a professional gardener, so we had apple, plum, and pear trees in the garden. The kids next door would sneak through the bushes to steal the plums and apples, which I don't blame them for. (I'd done the same thing when I was their age.)

The only thing separating the house from next door was a shared tunnel or alley to the back of the house. Dad had saved some rubber from the old house – he'd prised it up from the floors and recut it for the new house. That was his way.

The woman next door was younger than Dad, and after I'd decorated she came over and fell in love with the place. Which was natural; everybody did, who saw it. Dad used to polish the floor with a cream. Well, she loved it, and invited Dad to her house. But he said, *No thank you luv.* (When Mum died, Dad said to me: *No one will ever take her place.*) Still, she invited him to a party. She'd told the neighbours about the floor and so forth.

The day of the party, I told Dad to wear my suit. *Oh, they're too good for me* he said. —They're not too good for you! (He was always conscious of...well, of himself.) He had a good head of hair, my father, until his last days. And I got him a fresh set of teeth. —You could be a bleeding model, Dad. (I might have been fibbing a bit.)

Anyhow, he went to the party, but after 45-50 minutes he came back. —Is it over already, Dad?

—No, I took my leave of absence, son.

Sounds a bit grand, but he'd use phrases like that. Or 'I decided to sling him a deaf'un,' meaning to ignore someone saying something he didn't want to hear. That was his language, and Unkie's too.

I remember this old man used to come into the pub and drink by himself. One day, Dad asked why he was always alone. —Well, I don't have any friends.

So Dad invited him over. Now, my Dad was in the best group of people there – not in terms of living standards, but for fun. Dad had had trials for Aston Villa; his best pal was Ernie Horton, 6'3", who'd played with the great Tom Finney at Preston North End, who was the next name to Stanley Matthews. When Ernie'd injured his leg and was out of work, my Dad collected a lot of money for him; he never forgot that. But Dad idolized him, because of his soccer skills. He was captain of Clynes's, the best pub team in the area.

The old chap comes over, he offers to buy everyone a drink. —Keep your bleeding money to yourself, we pay for our own beer here. Well, occasionally someone will buy a drink, but whatever.

Another time, a few days later, Dad bumps into him again outside the pub. And the man insists: —Wally, let me buy you a drink next time. Please.

—You don't have to do that.

But the man says, almost apologizing, —I've got quite a bit of money, Wally.

Dad says, —What do you mean, you've got a lot of money? You can bleeding give it *me!* (Dad was joking, of course.)

And the man says, —I won the Irish Sweepstakes.

Dad says, —Alright then, come in.

After that, the man would send drinks over without saying who they were from, but of course they knew.

Dad had a phrase he'd use: 'I put him into touch.' Meaning, when you've got a winger coming down the line, you give him a nudge. Out of play, out of action. Same thing applies. When someone comes in, *poncing:* —Oh, could you let us have a *drink,* Wally. And you'd end up buying them a drink every week. *Poncing,* always asking for money. Someone does that, what'd you do? —Oh, I slung him a deaf'un and put him into touch. He was a *mumper.* (Meaning, he'd never get off your back.)

You don't hear that language anymore; these words are from a different era, another world. They were part of the education I got from Dad and Unkie.

My father was once helping a friend of his, a card sharp. He taught me how to pick an ace out, roll it down... It was how he earned his living on the trains. Someone would start a game, the card sharp stays solo, then one of the players sees him and invites him in... One thing leads to another. That's the *pull-in.*

As I say: another world, and it's a good thing I moved on from it. But I miss it sometimes.

Anyhow. After the war, the government leveled certain streets that had been bombed clear, bringing in bulldozers and steamrollers, flattening everything out. This chap I spoke of, who won the Sweepstakes, he only lived 300 yards from the pub. He said to my Dad, —Wally, if I should die, I want you to know where I put the money.

—No no, just tell your family...

—Well I've told *them,* they know. But I'm telling *you,* because I'm grateful for your friendship.

Dad told me as well.

We weren't waiting or hoping for him to pass on, don't get me wrong. But it was a strange thing to know. He was doing us a kindness, because Dad had brought him to his table and welcomed him.

The bulldozers came in and flattened his house completely, of course. Did he get his money out before he died? I've no idea.

It's what they call 'a curiosity.'

Anyhow, I asked Dad what happened at the party next door.

—Well son, they're talking about *insurance*. And where they want to be bleeding buried.

We were 200 yards from the largest cemetery in the area.

—I don't need that, son. Talking about death and so forth.

Dad lived another twenty years or so after that. He's buried in that cemetery, actually.

He preferred to *live* while he was alive, and I'm the same.

CHAPTER 9

The lads

I should tell you about Mooresy, shouldn't I.

After getting demobbed, when I moved back in with Dad, I was knocking about with Smoky Bacon. His family owned a pub in Moss Side, a rough district. Smoky used to serve behind the bar for his father. When I'd go, we'd play cribbage. A very good pub for entertaining. Smoky and I would go out of a weekend, Friday and Saturday, by bus and taxi. We'd go dancing: Belle Vue, the Ritz, Princess Road, Platt Lane.

We did well.

We played for a team called Burnage Villa, if I remember rightly. Definitely from Burnage, where Smoky lived with his mother and father. Smoky was adopted – a good-looking man, bigger than me, and played center-half. We both smoked, would drink a bit of beer. Wherever we'd go we'd get a few dances; we'd put on suits, look tidy. Quite the pair. If some women came over we'd split up, go our separate ways, but if it didn't pan out, we'd go to a nightclub together afterwards. It could get expensive, but Eric was never short of money, as his parents did quite well at the pub.

I had a bit of money, savings from selling extra fabric lengths on the side, but I was reluctant to – well, I never felt sure what would happen next. I was reluctant to *commit* to it, you might say. *It's never there until it's in your hand.*

Smoky and I had corresponded all during the war. He was with the Lancashire Fusilliers. A beautiful writer, where I was reluctant to write, but willing to, for my friends. Smoky came home a month earlier than me, as he was a month older, and he wrote to me before he left Trieste: 'They're wearing yellow and white socks now, even with suits. Dancing the be-bop-a-lula...'

I got home, bought a heavy tweed sports jacket, and finished up wearing the same thing as everyone else, a one-piece jacket with different-coloured lapels. I wore my hair in a 'D.A.,' a 'duck's arse,' combed together in the back. Crepe-soled shoes, so you didn't walk, you *bounced*. That might sound silly, but if you didn't have crepe-soled shoes, you couldn't dance the jive properly.

Once we went to Bellevue, a very large complex in the center of Manchester like a little Disneyworld, with a dance hall where they'd host competitions. I saw a heavyweight fight there in 1974, the American champion – and a motorbike championship, oddly enough. This particular night we came out, and there were three big fellows from Liverpool. They'd had a few beers; one of them started picking on me. Smoky said to leave me alone, so they asked if *he* wanted have a go. He was very polite: —Yeah, I'll take you on, certainly.

Smoky gave him a good hiding for me. I've never been a big guy, short and not very heavy. When I played for City against Blackburn Rovers as an amateur, Smoky was with me – and he was a far superior player to me. He was a defender, and played quite a few games for City. But like myself, he was more interested in having a few beers, sex, smoking and so forth.

And we looked out for each other. Put it this way: how many people promise to write you all through their two years in the service, and actually do it?

He wasn't actually named 'Smoky,' of course. His name was Eric, but with a name like Bacon you can't complain when your mates call you Smoky. There are plenty of Erics already; 'Smoky' is easier to remember.

Johnny Yarwood was 'Feet.' Crombie was 'Teeth.' McDonough was 'Diltch.' The #1 person was Grimsley, 'Grimmo': he was the cock of the school. There was Peter Amato, the Italian who used to put his finger into his mouth and making a popping sound with his cheek – he might just have been 'Amato,' come to think of it. Longbottom was 'Matty.' There was Shovelbottom as well, and his nickname was 'Shovey,' which you'll agree could have been much worse. Hoyles went by 'Yank.' Buckley was 'Patty.' Lyons was 'Butch.'

And I was 'Dutch' – which is certainly an easier name to live with than 'Teeth' or 'Diltch,' isn't it.

I was always good for a laugh, and George was very funny, but where Smoky and Arthur Colbridge were quite bright, George was like me. He was a truck driver, and used to have a horse and cart in the early days of that job.

Well: that was one way of surviving. Otherwise he wouldn't have been able to drink with the lads. Though in the long run you're better off drinking milk, I suppose.

I'd tell George what suits to buy, because you look out for each other where you're best able. For instance: I'd had my tweed suit made, and I said to George, —Why don't you have one made? You can wear it to the picnic. I won't have you coming to the picnic wearing the suit you wore last week; that's all right for the pub, but...

As you have hopefully *divined* by this point, we were planning a picnic.

Now to close the deal: —And I can fix you up with a girl. The girl I fancy, she's got a friend, tall like you with dark hair.

—You sure?

—Sure.

I liked to help out.

So down we went to Burton's, to get the suit made. Now, in those days the black men in Moss Side were wearing 'zoot suits,' these enormously baggy outfits with trousers that ballooned out from the belt and then got slim at the bottom.

George tried a coat on: fit him like a glove. —That's the one.

Now, you don't try trousers on, do you? There's no need. So we went away. A few days later, I had George meet me outside where I worked. He steps off the bus wearing a tie I'd chosen for him. I looked at the jacket: like a *glove*. There was hope for him after all. —Looks great, George.

I looked down.

The trousers, of course, were ballooning out like a parachute. They'd given him half of a zoot suit to wear.

The girl took one look at him and started laughing and that was that.

After a few beers he blamed me. Does that strike you as fair?

That picnic was where we met Billy Moore for the first time. (I told you I'd talk about Moorsey.) He'd brought a pack of guys from the foundry, a rough lot, and some of them were trying to pick fights with George in his bloody zoot suit. But Billy, being manager, let them know what was what: —*No need for all that, lads.*

Needless to say, the picnic ended perfectly. It's been raining, and this girl is sitting on a swing, and George has offered to push her. First push: no problem. Second push: George slips and falls flat on his back in this suit, underneath the swing, covered in mud, his trousers ballooning out around him like he was jumping out of a plane. It was the funniest thing I'd seen in my life.

Over the years we all became very close, George and Billy and me. How could we not? After all, everyone had made such a good first impression.

Another story about Billy Moore, since I don't want you thinking too highly of him:

We went camping in Scotland, in Lockerbie. The iron foundry where Mooresy was manager was a rough place to work. There were these two kids at the foundry who wanted to go fishing, so off we went. We took a tent, put it on the side of the stream, and then naturally we'd go to the local pub for a couple of pints. One of the lads was slower than the other. He bought a brand new rod and reel for the trip, fairly nice stuff. Now, Billy had done quite a bit of fishing, and still does, even in his later years.

So here we are in Scotland, and we're not catching any fish. And Billy says to the boy, —For Christ's sake, no wonder – that fishing rod's a jinx! Give it me, I'll use it!

And he gave the slower lad a tree branch with a piece of string on it, and took the new fishing rod off him. Billy must have felt he was getting the better deal, with a new rod.

The young guy caught a fish with the tree branch, of course.

Billy took it rather well: —No swapping back now, he said. I think he kept the fishing rod, but fair's fair, he did let the other lad keep the stick.

One day on the same trip, the lads had been on the whiskey. And the backwards fellow wanted to stay on and drink more with the other apprentice. It wasn't for us to say no. They were only 19 years of age, say. Now, we'd camped on the edge of the river. What Billy did was, he moved the tent, so that when you dived into the tent, you dived into the bleeding *river*. It was only a few feet deep, no danger. But the two of them were well drunk, and it sobered them right up. That's how Billy did things.

I phone him every other weekend, even now.

Billy was a good soccer player – but if you went past him too quick he'd kick you. He had a tremendous sense of humour, though I don't suppose that's *entirely* funny.

Mooresy and I went to a dance in Pickmere with a couple of others in the crowd. Today's United players would live in that area; it's the type of place you'd have the *local hunt*. Billy and I were together; the other two were both called Ronnie, one normal size, the other barely 5'2". They were pals – both engineers, I think. Eventually the Ronnies left for Australia or New Zealand to work away. But here they were, the two Ronnies, waiting at the dance hall when we arrived.

Billy and I saw two girls and agreed to go over and talk with them, as you do.

But! There was one girl who'd nodded to me, like *I'd like to dance with you.* So I left Billy to talk to that girl instead. By the time he said anything, I was already walking to the dance floor. What could I do, I fancied my chances – she'd *nodded,* after all. —I'll not be a minute, Bill.

Don't forget, though, Billy had the car. He let me have it afterward: —You left me stood there like a right bleeding idiot with two girls, one says 'Where's your partner?' And to see you dancing with this other girl, you put me right in the shit.

This is how he'd talk to me, can you *imagine.*

—Wally, I'll get my bleeding own back on you, you know.

So he *left* me at the dance hall in Pickmere, which is a long way from Manchester – it would have cost me a week's wages to get back in a taxi, and I didn't have a week to spare. I went to find the two Ronnies. The smaller one wasn't there. —What's happened, Wall?

—I think Bill's gone out with Ronnie, they must've took two birds home.

—Well, the creeping *bastards*.

So big (bigger) Ronnie and I left; he dropped me off where I lived. And of course, little Ronnie was left in Pickmere. Bill found out the next week, and the next time we all got together, he put some questions to me. —What happened? My pal Ronnie being left behind, etc., etc.

Big Ronnie was surprised. —What do you mean, left behind?

—Well, *you* didn't run him home, did you?

Indeed we had not.

Bill explained, —Well, I had to leave Wally, because...

Oh, he *had* to.

Neither of the Ronnies knew what had happened with Bill and me, and I wasn't about to clarify things, as I used to tell lies when I was younger. I don't anymore, mind you. But I did then. Plenty.

—Well, little Ronnie was left behind, says Billy. And he turns to me. —You creeping *bastard*, Wally, to do that to a pal of yours. He's smaller than you. He's got shorter *legs*.

—He's got shorter legs than anybody, hasn't he! You didn't want me walking home, did you? You left *me*, you creeping bastard.

This is how it was, how we spoke to each other. 'Creeping bastard' can be a term of endearment, so to speak. And it was all in fun – except to little Ronnie, I suppose.

I told you I'd been a little thief, after all, and the disreputable lifestyle never quite leaves your body.

Another time we heard there was a party on at Shay Brennan's. We'd been out, Mooresy and me, and we decided to go to the house. When we arrived, there was a light on upstairs – and then it went out. Mooresy says, —Oh, they don't want *us* to go to the party. So what we'll do is, *we'll get in anyhow.* Come on, Wally.

He put me on his shoulders so I could climb through this window and get into the house. The lights are out, they've closed the doors, they're *keeping us out of the party.* It hardly seemed sporting, and so here am I on Mooresy's shoulders.

I got into the window, and it's completely empty of course, because the party's happening *next* week. And then this bleeding Alsatian dog comes for me, barking, and I had to shut the bedroom door to keep it out. —Who's there?! —It's Wally, it's Wally!

They were in bed, of course. In the spirit of fellowship I added, —It's not just me, Mooresy's downstairs!

They never stopped laughing about it as long as I knew them.

A month later, I'd had too much to drink at one of their parties, and they set me down on the bed to sleep. And they put the *bloody dog* next to me in the bed, sleeping. So that when I woke up...

Good lads, all of them. A mad crowd.

All in all there were twenty or thirty of us. (You don't get crowds that big anymore, do you, with young people moving around so much.) We'd head to the Oaks pub in Chorlton-cum-Hardy, which Georgie Wilson and I could walk to. I'd take him to the dances that I could get to, when I was in textiles. I'd introduce him, help him get a bird. He was a marvelous singer, could croon like Sinatra. Don't get me wrong, he didn't always know the words, but when he sang...

We'd all get done up properly, looking smart – some of the crowd had a tailor, Abie Sacks, not well-known but excellent. Mine was Olaf Schultz from the center of town. Shay Brennan and Johnny Dougherty had money, playing for United; Johnny's brother Ernie was there as well.

There was a big entertainment room at the Oaks, a 'vault' – a room for men only – and the lounge for men and women. George would start giving a song, and he'd get a lot of girls coming. But he had an impediment in his speech. The day he got married, when I was best man, I had a 14oz navy blue suit on, and he had on a suit from Harry Davis. In the chapel, the priest asked, —Do you take this woman to be your lawful wedded wife?

Now, when George was singing, he never made a mistake. Absolutely *fluent*. But at the wedding he was sweating cobs, nervous. —Do you take this woman...?

So he started stammering a bit. —I, I, I...

At the Oaks, he'd finish singing, and come out into the crowd. If a girl approached him and he stuttered, I'd mouth the words for him, to help out, until he could get them out himself. The longer he spoke to the girl, the more confident he got, and the stammer disappeared entirely – but he needed a bit of a push at first. I was glad to help.

So naturally, as best man at the wedding, I did the same. I leaned over and said, —I will!

I wonder if *I'm* actually married to his wife as a result.

At the Oaks we'd point out to the landlady that it was a lot of work for us to get there – the expense, the time. And she appreciated the business. She said to us, —Well, there's two pints for each of you, when you show up.

Two pints! Some of them, that was just the *start* to the night, but that would last me the entire evening, until we went to the late clubs. I said to the landlady, quite craftily I thought, —You know, there's a lot of young ladies come here to just hear George. Let's talk *finances*...

—All right, Wally, she said. I figured we'd hit the big time. And this was her generous offer: —Let's make it *four* pints.

So George and I got four beers each as long as he was singing, and I was his manager. But of course I didn't want four *beers*. I'd have my two for the night and call out as I left, —Don't forget you owe me two next time...

Then George and I would come back in the week and drink the rest of our fee, which never took long.

You know, out of all of us in the old district, nobody's done better than Georgie Wilson. Smashing fellow.

I remember the clubs, our 'scene': Piccadilly, Chez Joey, the Stork Club. Eli Rose owned the Stork Club and Chez Joey; years later, he *voluntarily* went to Australia, if you can believe that, and in a bit of a hurry. He won on a horse at 33-1, and apparently he had to move quickly.

At the Stork Club, you'd see Jackie Blancheflower who played for United... His wife, Jean Parker, used to sing there. Jackie Blancheflower survived Munich, you know.

When I tell a story about Manchester, I can't help but remember all the other stories I have about the city, the people.

I remember Tony Hulme. The smartest human being I've ever seen – smartest-dressed, I mean. They used to call him 'Mr Immaculate.' I recollect bumping into him outside the Palace Theatre in Manchester, across the road from Tootal. Tony Hulme was outside with a beautiful blonde woman, who I assumed was from the cabaret. I saw her – but he's the one I remember, so to speak. He had that charisma.

Tony made it to TV, but never did well there. He had such a babyish face. And an effeminate manner, in the 50s, wasn't looked on the same way as it is now.

I bumped into Norman Wisdom, who was the biggest comedy star in England in his time, making movies for J Arthur Rank. He played a couple of instruments as well...

There was a place called the King Kong, or more likely the Hong Kong, a Chinese restaurant down the street from his cabaret. One of the first Chinese restaurants any of us knew about. They were accused of cooking mice years later, and putting them in the food. Of course you hear that about any Chinese restaurant, don't you, but it was the first I'd been to, and that story stopped me going there. Anyhow, I went there once with Smoky Bacon, and had had too much to drink, and fell asleep on the toilet. Smoky came looking for me, banged the door open (breaking the door), and my *head* must have been resting against it, because he knocked me clean off the toilet. I ended up even more unconscious than I already was.

They revived me eventually.

We were with another guy that night; we'd all gotten demobbed at the same time. He used to smoke a pipe. We'd tease him: 'What are you, a detective?' He thought it would get him a woman. Absolutely *ridiculous*.

Though I think it worked, actually.

Just to the side of the Palace Theatre was Whitworth Street, and across the street was the Insurance Building, one of the biggest buildings in the north.

In the early 50s, there was an Irish comedian at a comedy club on Whitworth Street, Dave Allen, who wore a black evening suit and tails. The stage was surrounded by a trough, and in the trough was 8-10" of water, with *baby alligators* in it, swimming around. He was doing his cabaret performance, and he'd sit on a stool on the stage, half-casual. An attractive, well dressed woman came in, obviously intoxicated. She walked straight up to him and sat down at the edge of the stage...right on the side of the trough.

Dave Allen stopped completely, in the middle of a joke. You could see perspiration running down his face. She was leaning, swaying, with her hands in the trough. Now, these were only *baby* alligators, but I wouldn't like to be bitten by one.

The worry was that she would *fall in*, you see. He called the attendants to get rid of her, and they removed her. Back to the jokes, and all that. But I'll never forget this: I've never seen such fear on a performer's face as I saw that night. That was the first night of the club.

A 'hard act to follow,' you might say.

J. Arthur Rank made a movie at the Insurance Building, and everyone in the area turned out to see it on their lunchtime. It was a little thing, but it mattered – seeing our city on the screen.

At the side of Tootal Broadhurst and Lee was a large canal, and we'd go swimming in it, with the dead rats and everything. It was a swimming pool's width. I could do a dog paddle across it, the most I can manage in terms of swimming. The trouble was, you needed a bath *after* you went in the canal. There was a tap where you could shower off.

...

I remember something else as well.

You know, Grimmo's little nephew drowned in that canal. I remember being on the bus, going home from work, and reading about it in the paper. I had to see Grimmo after that. I think the lad's name was Keddy. I couldn't stop crying.

Grimmo was so upset. Keddy *idolized* him. He was 8 or 10 years old.

The memory comes back to me suddenly, and I don't want to dwell on it, even to tell the story. But you can't separate your memories that way. I carry them all with me.

I don't wish to end with a sad story.

I had a good life after the war, all things considered. But eventually it was time to move on.

I know I told you this wasn't a book of *criminality* but que sera sera.

I'd started work at Provident Clothing Company, on the business side of things. My friend Bob's mum worked for the company, and she said it would be marvelous work: decent money, the assistant manager's job.

I'd bought a new Italian scooter, a 'Vespa.' (Do they still exist? I've never seen one in Ellicottville, anyhow.) The very day I bought it, I'd gone riding through Piccadilly in Manchester, which was bustling with activity. There were two stone lions facing each other, with water coming out of their mouths. Quite old-fashioned... No matter. I was riding home in the rain after picking up the scooter someplace out of town. A policeman was directing the traffic – there were no lights, of course; *primitive* – and he put his hand down quickly to signal stop. But I saw him too late, and was already heading through the traffic circle.

So as he put his arm out, naturally I went under his arm, as one does. Not a very nice thing to do, I admit, but I figured it was better to duck under him than to brake quickly on this new bike. I might fall over!

I should mention that I'd never ridden a scooter before in my life.

So I went under his arm. And he turned and blew the whistle, blew and blew. I turned around and came back. The policeman had opinions: —You went underneath my arm!

—Well, you was a *bit* late putting it down, I said.

—And you've just done a U-turn on a one-way street!

—Hang on, if I'd've carried on, you would've done me for trying to escape. This is a new bike, I could have been killed, you know!

Despite my attempts at using logic and reason, they fined me £20. Quite a lot of money.

In the coming weeks, I sent them two postal orders for £10 each, addressed to Strangeways prison. (You might recall I'd already had some trouble with Strangeways.)

As I say, I was working for the Provident Clothing Company, which is why I bought the bike in the first place. I certainly couldn't afford a car. I worked directly with the head man and Bob's mum, the head lady. We worked on the top floor of the building; on the bottom floor was Ames's cake shoppe, and in between was a Scottish lady named Margot who did hairdressing. For any readers joining in late, I'll reiterate: *black curly hair* I had, and so with her being in the trade, between one thing and another we'd had an affair.

The Provident Clothing Company gave loans to employees, with conditions: you could only spend at certain places. You'd pay well more than £20 back, of course – £2 a week, a pound a week after that.

We had a wooden staircase, so you could always hear anyone coming up the top flight of stairs. And one day we heard this pounding on the stairs. I was with the manager, dressed well as always.

In come two police officers. —Walter Holland?

—Yes sir, that's me.

—We have a warrant for your arrest.

Oh, very dramatic.

—You have not paid a bill for etc., etc., etc.

They put me in handcuffs and marched me down the stairs.

As you might expect, the girl in the cake shoppe, I'd been going out with her as well. So imagine me marching first by the hairdresser, then the cake shoppe – one minute I'm in love with two girls, the next minute I'm leaving the premises in handcuffs.

They put me in a Black Mariah and hauled me down to the police station, near where City's coaching ground is at Platt Field. They put me in a cell with somebody who killed a man the night before. Perhaps the police thought we'd get along.

Next thing, he's mopping the floor. And he turns to me and says, —*You'd* better do this.

—Oh, no. If they've asked *you* to do the job, you do it. (I didn't wish to interfere.)

The police came in. I assumed they were there to keep everyone safe. No. —You'll have to do the cleaning, now, Holland.

Bad enough the Crown has cheated me out of two girlfriends in a day, now I'm helping a murderer mop the *floor* on top of everything else.

After about thirty minutes, a police van came to take me down to Strangeways, in Deansgate. It was exactly opposite the place where I'd had my medical exam a few years before, when I went into the army. We entered the main offices. —I need to see a senior person, I said. —I sent the money *months* ago...well, a while ago. Two ten pound notes. Matter of fact, I've got the *receipts*.

They took this well: —You should've *showed* us those at the beginning.

—I never gave it a thought. I was in handcuffs, and *two* of my girlfriends were on the first and second floors. It's embarrassing – and I'd like you to apologize.

The Crown did not apologize.

—No, you will be arrested now.

In this situation you often hear a piece of advice: 'Keep Calm and Carry On.'

I asked to see the top person.

So the clerk of the courts came in. I showed him the receipts for the postal orders. —Just one moment, he said.

—So it seems these are two postal orders.

—'*Course* they bloody are! I *told* these...

—Did you send these?

—Of *course* I did!

—Well, you never signed them. You've left your name off.

Deansgate is quite a long way from home. It's a long way before you can even get on the *bus*. And for obvious reasons I hadn't come on my scooter – but the Crown did not, in fact, give me a lift home. They just let me outside the bleeding prison wall.

A smashing day.

I was arrested in Paris not long after, on suspicion of murdering a policeman – another *unfounded* charge I might add, and totally unrelated.

If you see me having a glass of wine at Dina's of a weekend, please don't be afraid. All this disreputable business is in the past.

CHAPTER 10

Football

The greatest player I ever saw with my own two eyes was Georgie Best.

You talk about *Messi*. Well, Best wasn't as good a player as Messi, though he was better for his team, in a way. As I *remember*. What Messi has that Best didn't have was his distribution, which makes him so much more a complete player. But by the same token, Best seemed a better defender. '*But I digress.*'

...

Actually, I'll stick with the digression for a moment; this is my memoir, after all. You should be grateful the entire book isn't about Manchester United.

Have I told you I'm a United supporter? I've loved United longer than I've loved any living person, if you can believe that.

(Yes, of course it's love, you can love a team. And you can actually dislike somebody you don't even know. Take the Liverpool captain, for instance. I can't stand the *sight* of him. The man's done nothing wrong to me – am I so unusual to think that way? I think we're *all* like that, with some people.)

The biggest name of my time was the Moscow Dynamos. They were a fabulous team in the early 50s. There were great English players, of course – well, *we* thought they were great players. The mentality that English people had: we thought the

English team was great, world class, but we were deceived. We were *all* living in a dreamland, it turns out.

The Russians came down and *pissed* on us, I think it was 5-3. We learned something by it.

I remember United winning the Cup in 1948. Well, I'll never forget. I'll tell you the entire team, actually: Crompton, Carey, Ashton; Anderson, Chilton, Cockburn; Delaney, Morris, Rowley, Pearson, and Mitten. Warner did not play; there was another young person took his place.

My eldest son tells me I should mention, here, that I didn't look those names up. But it's no big deal, really; I wouldn't forget my own name, and I wouldn't forget their names either.

Charlie Mitten was left-footed, so he played left wing. My best pal Albert Scanlon took his position over. (Charlie Mitten was his uncle!) In those days, there was a place called Bogotá. Out in the wilds! They wanted Charlie Mitten to go out there and play. And he went. It may have been toward the end of his career. They were paying him a lot of money, maybe three times what he was making in England. But after a short time he was forbidden from playing abroad because he had a contract with United, and he came home. This was the start of drafting out the English players. Denis Law, Reed who I played with, went to an Italian club. I think that was in the late 50s.

There's too much money now. It changes things. Take Billy Meredith, who played for City and United. He worked down the *mines* as well – the best player in Britain would come out of the mines on a Saturday and play for City at Maine Road. He probably made a good wage, but he still had to work. The disparity between those days and today is extraordinary. Leicester won the Premiership a couple of years ago, a wonderful story; they probably made hundreds of millions of pounds.

Even Smoky, who played semi-professionally, would only get *expenses* and a little more. Money was hard to come by, even with great international players. It used to be something that it isn't, anymore. That's why Charlie Mitten went to play for Bogotá, so he could earn a decent wage. The club owners made all the money. Three quarters of the ground was people standing, and seats available only if you could afford them...

Of course, it's not only the money that's changed. Today you've got Spanish, Bangladeshi, Germans, Africans, everyone, all playing in the same leagues. (And play marvelous football as well.) That wasn't the case in those years. So when you talk about the Busby Babes – young boys, 18, 20 – to play in the First Division, which wasn't called the Premier League then... When I talk about Georgie Best, you have to understand what I mean. In *those* years, Georgie Best was the best we'd ever had, with a soccer ball. Well, of course you had Puskás and di Stéfano, the great center-forward from Real Madrid, and Kopa on the left wing. But that's different, as far as I'm concerned.

Georgie Best, the Busby Babes, they were *ours*.

United innovated in putting young blood into the team. The Busby Babes were so *young*. And one of the greatest players ever was Duncan Edwards. Eighteen years of age. He was a *colossus*. It was like Gulliver in Lilliput to see him on the pitch.

Edwards was a left half, what you'd now call a 'midfielder.' Eighteen, and he played for England a few times, even at that age. The youngest ever to do so. You'd see him come onto the field, and his thighs were twice the size of a normal player's...

When the Munich disaster occurred, Duncan Edwards didn't die straight away. He died within the week, along with twenty-two other people. He was 21 years old. They couldn't save him. That was February 1958.

There's something I remember:

You'd get a paper on a Sunday night. It was called the *Evening Chronicle* if I remember right. You could get an early edition on a Saturday, with the 'football pink,' pages of football news. You had the *News of the World*, the *Empire News,* the *Sunday Mail*. But the *Chronicle*, if I remember correctly, the headline was: 'The World Stood Still for United.'

And what it meant was, every team in the country, all over the world, gave a minute's silence to Manchester United, and stood on the line with their heads bowed.

These were young kids. They were only boys, some of them, come from different parts of Britain. A pal of mine, Johnny Doherty, who I knew well later on, he played for the Busby Babes. And Albert, of course. 'The World Stood Still.'

In Manchester, the pubs closed, there were no buses. The lights of the buildings, the cinemas, they were all out; people stayed in, and those you saw walking had their heads down. There was...a silence. It was like the aftermath of the Blitz. The sirens died down, and there was only silence.

Now I want to tell you about Lloyds Celtic.

George was center-half and Grimmo was inside forward. Two of the lads passed away quite early in their lives, including the goalkeeper Bradford, who had a brother called Frank. Frank was the twelfth or thirteenth man, always waiting to get a game, willing to play for anybody. You need guys like that.

We had one coach who, if you got injured, he'd come onto the field with a Guinness.

—This is the best thing in the world, he'd say.

You know, I *think* he was an alcoholic.

The first year was our best ever. We won thirty-one games on the trot. We continued for years after, but it was never quite the same. Bradford passed away after the first or second year.

Brian Lillis and Johnny Moores were at fullback. Johnny played for Medlock Rovers as well. He got married; needless to say, he gave up playing after that.

On the halfback line was Yank, one of the best we ever had. He was only small, but nobody would get past him. A tremendously talented young man. George at center-half was quite tall, with a strong header. Now, if he made a good tackle in the first minute, the rest of the game he would be carried by his ego. And it was the same with his singing: if the first song went down well, he was the best singer in the world. But if it didn't, it made him nervous, and he'd stammer. He alternated between supreme confidence and total uncertainty.

Cobo was right half, Arthur Colbridge. He had a stroke a few years ago. Yank was captain – he passed away. In later years he'd been a great friend to Grimmo, after I moved away. I played on the left wing; the guy on the right wing wasn't as two-footed as me. I should have played wing half, that was my position, but – not wanting to sound egotistical – I was better than quite a few of them. No better than Yank or Grimmo or Joe Lambert, the inside forward, mind you.

The center forward was a lad called Peter Blaney, who worked with Smoky years later, when Smoky's life was on the rocks a bit. They worked on the railway together and he got to know Eric as well as I did.

I can't remember who played outside right, actually. Which may seem like a small thing to you, but it isn't to me.

Ricky Roe was center forward – he had the hardest shot that I've ever encountered in soccer. If Ricky hit it from twelve yards out there was *nothing* the keeper could do; if he put his hands on the ball he'd end up holding it at the back of the net, that's how strong Ricky was. Ricky died quite early as well, I don't know why, and so did Joe Lambert. Joe and I were pals at school together, but he got egotistical – a good player, though. He was also at Maine Road for a while. He had a chip on his shoulder, mostly about soccer. (Neither of us was good looking enough to have a chip on our shoulders about *that*, although – I'm not sure if I've mentioned this – I did have a fine head of black curly hair.)

I went to a couple of dances with Joe Lambert, and was there when he met his wife-to-be. She came in from the country, and had a very attractive blonde friend whom I remember quite well. When I say 'country,' this is what I mean:

English: Are you going up the hill?

Country: Ehyoo gon oopill?

It was its own jargon. I *love* it, there's nothing wrong with it, but Joe's two girls, they both spoke like that. A bit hard to figure out what we're talking about. And the blonde girl had false teeth. She was only about twenty. When you kissed her, the wind would whistle through her teeth. So I only ever did that once. She was a lovely girl and I wished her well, though.

Joe would use the same tailor as me, Harry Davis; we'd get suits on credit. Harry's was a well-known name all over the north of England.

Joe had a brother who played for us occasionally. He was solid as granite, great broad shoulders, stocky; Grimmo, Ricky, and Brian had a bit of size to them. Brian was inclined to be a bit fat, actually. The rest of us, a good meal could've killed us.

I don't know why I tell you about that. But if I don't, who will? And if not this, what will I tell you? This is what *life* is: who you're with, what you do together. I was with my friends, and we won thirty-one games on the trot. And now they're almost all gone.

Arthur Colbridge is still alive, Johnny Moores, George Wilson, and myself. I believe we're the last.

Arthur's wife had a very beautiful sister called Esther, who lived up towards the nicer side of Moss Side. One of my first loves, as a grown man. Arthur's wife – I think her name was Vicki – she said her sister had seen me playing soccer and so forth, and wanted to meet me. We went out, and for me she would've been #1, back then. But she lived *miles* away, near where City played at Maine Road. It's a long way; there are buses running that way, but you get fed up with riding the bus. So I dropped off the relationship.

Years later, I saw Brian Lillis, the fullback, for his 50th wedding anniversary. He'd married one of the twins. Arthur and his wife came to the party – you could see he was getting old – and Vicki lit into me a bit about Esther, why did I break up with her and all that.

—I know! I said. —By the way, what happened to her?

—She's had a rough time, she said, and told me about it. —But I'll tell you something. She never got over losing you. She really wanted to marry you.

—I would've done! But she lived such a long way off...

It's a nice feeling and a sad story at once, if you take my meaning. To know she had the same feelings for me that I had for her.

Brian Lillis finished up living in Hayfield, come to think of it. And dying there as well – his family owned a pub, and it went to him.

I never did see Esther after things ended.

Now, look. I wasn't going to be getting on a bus at 11:00 of a night, and then *hoping* to get a bus back in the middle of the night. You wouldn't chance that.

All the same, as I sit in my apartment in Ellicottville I sometimes think back on old girlfriends with curiosity: *I wonder what happened to her?* With girls it was totally different than with my friends; we wouldn't usually stay in touch afterward.

The best move I ever made was when I allowed Cata to capture me. I couldn't believe that someone of that intelligence would...well. She had a tremendous humour about her. She was bright, vibrant, everything.

It only makes sense to talk about women in a chapter about football – when a game has meant everything to you for eighty years, it makes sense; when you talk about football, you can talk about anything. But if it's all the same, I'll tell you about Cata later. I prefer to hold onto our story a bit longer.

Dad

I've no pictures of Mum,
I'm afraid.

At the ordnance depot
Kure, 1953

The food was better
abroad –
with Jackie Sutherland
and John Slater

Bob Martin and myself in Hong Kong

Two years was enough, I think

I promise I spent it responsibly

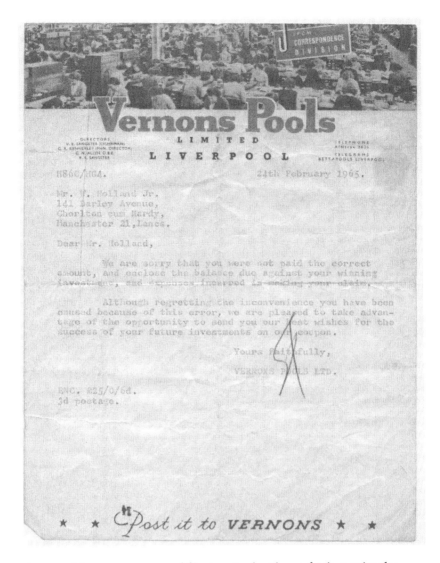

A rare thing to see a gambling organization admit a mistake like this

George Wilson and 'your humble narrator,'
at George's wedding

In Istanbul with BEA. I don't think the senior stewardess at right quite approved. I had no complaints

Keeping spirits up: The Bristol Hotel

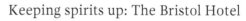

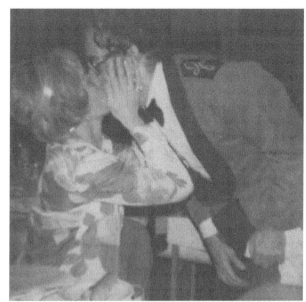

You can't
blame her

The night I danced onstage with the Supremes – a good night
for them, I think

I'm told they miss me in the Caribbean

Chatting with the Governor

¿Donde está el baño?

The way we were...

...and the way we are now

Veteran's Day in
Ellicottville,
presented with an
American flag. A
generous gift

We showbiz people call this sort of thing a 'head shot': From our recent production of *One Flew Over the Cuckoo's Nest*

Why didn't you tell me my hair had gone grey?

CHAPTER 11

Newquay (and Interpol)

In 1965 I started working in Newquay, Cornwall, as a bartender and waiter. I worked there through the 1973 summer season, with offseasons in Manchester and Lancashire, and a brief interlude away at my dream job.

In 1966 I had a violent disagreement with a swan.

'Like sands through the hourglass, so are the days of our lives...'

I started off at a cabaret in Newquay, Bernard Manning's place, though his brother ran the club. I worked every night, all season – they'd pay us a pound a night, but better still, I got to work with the top comedians in England – though if you ask them, I'd like to think they'll tell you they were lucky to work with *me*.

Bernard Manning was the most disgusting comedian I'd ever heard. But I thought he was also the funniest. He did the command performance for the queen, you know, which was good of her. Manning became a multimillionaire, but he still lived in the same sort of working-class house that we used to have during the war. He did a lot for charity, was a City supporter. Nobody's perfect. He wanted to be famous, but his language was always down low. In his club, he'd imitate Prince Philip shaking his hand: —Hello, Mr Manning. My God, how *much* I enjoyed your comedy!

And Manning would say in response, —Oh, *bollocks*. (It was no small thing, to make fun of the royal family like that. It was his way of letting us know he was still one of us, so to speak.)

In his club he'd say, —I have two clean jokes for you tonight, only two, *two* only... And then he'd say, —Now, have I mentioned the word 'bollocks?'

When a woman came into the club in a white dress, he'd torture her a bit. —Oh good Jesus, luv. You're living on memories... Aye-aye, luv, when you're laughing like that your *tits* are going up and down.

He'd do this to normal people coming into the club. It was funny – but also a bit over the top. Cruel, even. And maybe that's something to do with where he came from, and stayed.

How I ended up at the cabaret

I was asked to go to the cabaret by this guy I played soccer with. I'd been an apprentice in textiles, and so forth; I had my own trade. He said, —Come on down, you'll work every night.

That sounded alright. I'd never been a waiter, but I'd worked at a bar at Manchester University, part-time, making money on the side. I was ready for a change; a textile plant isn't the liveliest place, and I wanted to meet new people, keep moving.

So I took the job, and went down to the cabaret before the season started.

One of the bartenders came from the Embassy club in Manchester, where Bernard and Frank Manning had been. He was accustomed to a certain way of doing things; when I brought cash over to the bar for someone's drink, he'd say, —Don't bother about putting the cash down, just *flow away* with it.

Meaning: *let's you and me steal the cash.* But that meant being a thief, and I was done with that. I told him no way. He had the same arrangement with a couple of other waiters, and in the end they got caught. No matter.

We had a casino section, packed every night, with a good-looking Indian guy who brought girls in. It was the top place in Newquay.

After my first year in Newquay, I had enough experience to work as a bar manager at the Bristol hotel, which wouldn't allow the Beatles or Stones to stay inside. Drugs and such – it was a wealthy crowd at the Bristol, and they didn't want young people around making trouble.

It was a night job, of course, so I had the daytime hours to myself. I stayed in a little concrete house at the back of a guest-house. The lady who owned the place was a navy pilot, Millie Cooke, married to a ship's captain. There was room for five guests, and I used to serve breakfast for them of a morning, and slept at the back no charge, with a window by the bed. I made even more money waiting on people in the guest-house, and of a lunchtime, I could go work in one of the hotel bars in town if need be – I had a good name, I was honest.

Now, years later on the *Queen Elizabeth* I got to work with an absolutely professional Spanish waiter. I argued with him on one occasion, but realized that I'd die without him, workwise, and quickly made it up with him; we became good friends. I got the sense that for a lot of the Spanish and Italian boys I met on the ship, being a waiter wasn't just a job they took on. They were proud of it – it was a way of life, creating this experience for people coming in to the restaurant. Other people talk about being a doctor, an attorney, soldier, police, but for most of us waiting tables is something you'd just end up doing, to get a bit of work. But to have a uniform, to treat people with respect and be treated the same because of your professionalism, is something special, no matter what job you're in.

The guys and girls in Newquay that I was working with, though, a lot of them had never done that kind of work before. Like me. Having worked in the cabaret and the bar at the university, I knew my way around a little bit, but it wasn't the same as making it your *trade*.

Of course, I had other things going for me. Since I was showing up before everyone else, before the season started, I had a proper suntan right at the start. One day you're an albino, the next day you're brown as a walnut. So when the girls turned up, I was the maître d', with black curly hair and a nice tan, and as the oldest and the most experienced I was the one they'd come to with questions. So that was alright.

Honestly, it was like a paid vacation for four and a half months.

I was in my thirties, though, while most of the people working in town were 18, 20. It's not as if people were expecting to go to university – not like with my sons, where there was no chance they *wouldn't* go. Someone might ask today: *Where did you go to school?* Well, in my day half of us never knew! We'd go to whatever school was nearest where we lived, if we went at all.

There were quite a few Liverpool lads there, including Frankie Jones, who I still phone from time to time. We all worked at different places in town, but we'd all meet up together at the disco of a Saturday night, and dress up. Eventually I started coming along.

How could I not? Motown was in – the greatest music ever made.

Working at the cabaret, I'd work for four months without a real night off during the week, so getting to meet up on a Saturday was a special feeling.

It was really something – the time, of course, the 60s, but also the place. You'd walk out of the hotel and be two hundred yards from the beach, with bars and hotels all along that you could visit. I knew all the other bartenders and hotel staff, so we'd always say hi to one another. I don't want to go on about women and so forth, but – we were young together, without a care in the world.

Newquay was like a party every day. Every day someone new would come to the hotel for lunch, and as the most experienced I'd be assigned to serve them all. And I'm not that good a waiter, frankly, but I was clean and honest and could tell a joke. (I think I still can, but I suppose that's for you to judge.)

With the cabaret being the best place in town, a lot of the wait staff at other places in town would come by at night. So here I am, on the beach *all day*, with a good suntan, black curly hair, a soccer player. Not bad. People knew me, even if I didn't know them – it's a bit like that in Ellicottville now, though my hair's no longer black or curly, nor is it on my head for the most part anymore. But there's that same feeling, of being in a small world of your own.

And there *were* women, of course. I keep telling you how lucky I've been...

That said, it wasn't all *good* luck. I got engaged as well.

Her name was Vicky. She was Irish, blonde. I was working at the cabaret. If the comedians needed someone to go on, I was the one they called up. I made a pound a night in wages, but the performers would give half a quid to come on and act the fool or whatever. Vicky was with a group of girls that had come down from a restaurant in the village. We had lunch, got to know each other, walked on the beach in the sun.

I asked quite nicely, and she said yes quite nicely, and we got engaged.

Then I found out, from one of the girls at the restaurant where she worked, that she'd gotten a bit involved with the chef where she worked.

Well, one night I pretended to be sick, and took a night off work. That night I took her to every place in town, the best bars, the best hotel. There was nobody better known in the village than me. Onstage at the cabaret, playing soccer, on the beach – everybody in the village recognized us. There was no need to say anything.

Vicky said, —Wow, you're well-known in town.

—Don't knock that ring, I said. —It's coming off tonight.

Still, that wasn't the end of it.

One evening, before I went in to work, I saw her passing the door of the place where I was eating. —Hi, how are you?

She looked miserable. She'd been crying. —Why have you been crying?

—Everybody's turned against me.

I could understand that.

She said, —And I've told my mum and dad that you're coming home with me.

Well, I'd also told *my* father that Vicky was coming home with me, that we were engaged. So I said, —I'll go home with you, stay a couple of days, you can borrow the ring, so you can ease it off for them.

It seemed like the right thing to do.

I left the ring with her after I said goodbye to Vicky's family, and told her she could tell them *she* broke it off, if she wanted.

The day I left, I had a bet on the horses, and backed three winners, winning quite a lot of money, thirty or forty quid. I had a beautiful wool suit on, with subtle orange and grey stripes; Frank Manning had sold it to me for £5 after paying £20 for it. Looked better on me than it did on him. (It's a good job it did, since it was the only suit I had with me.)

Well, there I was, my best suit on, backed three winners, I'd gotten out of a bad situation with Vicky, and her two beautiful sisters were being terribly kind to me on my way out.

I suppose it worked out for the best.

Women are always coming up to me and kissing me, you know, even though I'm going a *bit* grey.

I hate to disappoint people, but sometimes I have *places to be*.

Sometimes you end up in prison.

I know I've told you that already, but as my son Wally says, it is 'unexpectedly relevant' at this point in the story.

At the end of one season, some friends and I decided to go to the Canary Islands. I went with a chap called Joe Hayes – well, Keith, but we called him Joe, as you do – and five girls. We had quite a bit of money saved from the season – at first. We were there for five weeks after working the entire season without a day off; that's five months of straight work! And we stayed in an old penthouse, cheap.

It wasn't all grand, though: I'd taken my scooter down to Cornwall with me for the season, and driving one day I'd hit a stone, which hit me underneath my right eye. I already had a scar under my *left* eye, from back when I was evacuated. For some reason I'd had my hair shaved off. Being in the desert, I was as brown as a loaf of bread. But the desert wears on you, a bit...

Meanwhile, back in London—

(That's the sort of thing you get to write in a memoir, even if it sounds a bit silly. 'Meanwhile, in Tokyo...' 'Meanwhile, on a ship in the Caribbean...' If you get the chance to write one yourself, no one's stopping you. Send me a copy.)

At any rate:

Meanwhile, back in London, there were two police officers murdered. The police were out looking for the one who'd done it, a man named Harry Roberts. A real criminal.

I mentioned there were *five* girls, correct? Well, Joe and I ran out of money. We had to get back to England – we had enough between us to get over to France, but only just – then we had to hitchhike to Paris. We were both young, but I was recovering from the blow underneath my eye. And with my hair shaved off, and having lost quite a bit of weight in the desert – well, imagine how I looked.

First things first, some food: I found fifteen francs on the ground just as we got off the ferry in the south of France.[3] So off we go. We managed to purchase a long French loaf and some cheese. We're just getting from A to B, you see? That's how we were, always moving, going. We took the food to a spot near a lake, with swans floating on the surface, a lovely place for a rest. And of course one of us dropped the loaf into the lake, and a bleeding swan flew over to get it. A *scuffle* ensued – after all, that was all we had, not even a bit of cheese.

Our plan was to hitchhike, and it worked out at first. An Italian woman, about to give birth, was driving with her mother in a little Fiat. She stopped the car, moved the luggage to the

---

[3] The ship was called the *Ne Plus Ultra*. I don't speak French or Latin, so I can't tell you offhand what it means; all I know is that it didn't sink on the way.

roof, and gave us a lift. (I've had good luck with Italians in general.)

But when we get to Paris, it appears our luck's run out. We get to the center of city, but only just: the money's gone, neither of us speaks the language, and my black curly hair's all gone. And of course the five girls are *miles* away.

Have you ever seen *Waiting for Godot?*[4] I said to Joe, —We can't go on like this.

The new plan was to find a police station or the British Consulate and ask for a bit of credit or some help, to avoid being picked up for loitering. Sensible, no? Well, we get to a police station. The officer asks for my documentation, I show it to him.

He says, —Will you come this way, sir?

I was quite happy to do so.

—We'd like to ask you a few questions.

This 'gave me pause,' as they say.

—Is this your passport?

—Yes.

—You are Harry Roberts.

—No I'm not.

They were 'inclined to see things differently.'

So now, apparently, Interpol has me behind bars in Paris.

I had no idea who Harry Roberts was, but at that point I was starting to *feel* like him. At least there wasn't a murderer in the cell with me for a change.

They made some inquiries, contacted the embassy and so forth. I was there for two hours. Joe was trying to help: —He's not bloody Harry Roberts!

---

[4] Now that we've gotten to know each other, I can tell you a secret: this is my son's joke, not mine. I won't tell you whether I've seen *Waiting for Godot* either.

So they had to calm *him* down, as he was getting a bit excited. Still, justice was served in the end:

—Alright, Mr Holland, we have confirmed that you are *not* Harry Roberts.

They showed me a photograph of him. Actually, it's not so much that I looked like him as that *he* was the spitting image of *me*. At that moment Harry Roberts was hiding in the bushes in Surrey, I believe. They captured him soon enough.

—Anyhow, Mr Holland, as compensation we'll make travel arrangements for you and your...colleague. And food vouchers, to get you back to England.

Vive la France, is that the expression?

I've been back to Paris a few times, with the airlines and with my old flatmates Nobby and Colin. I love it: lights, cafes, boulevards. *Life* everywhere. I think that's why I love Chicago, actually – it has the same bustling feeling.

But then, I look out my window here at home, at a little field of green grass and some trees, and I'm not thinking of going anywhere. I'm just grateful to be alive, to be *here*. And in those days, the Sixties, I felt the same, in a way: a bit of money in my pocket (usually), a bit of traveling, some women to talk to, no worries at all – as long as you kept moving. You have to be grateful, I think, no matter where you are. Or how can you bear it?

At any rate, the Sixties were better than the Fifties, for me. No one sent me to a war, for one thing.

But just when things were going well, I got my dream job.

CHAPTER 12

Flying

For a brief time in 1965 I wore a different sort of uniform –
quite a nice one as well. I do love a double-breasted jacket. I was
a steward with British European Airways: BEA.

The lad who helped me get the job, Cobo from Lloyds Celtic,
suggested that I put in the application.

—Tell them you've got bar experience, he said. I was 31 years
of age.

They did the interview at the airport in Manchester.

I wore a trilby, a nice raincoat, and a new brown tweed suit
that I'd had made. I couldn't afford things like that any old time,
but for the interview you want to put your best foot forward.
Most of the guys there were 21 or 22; I was 31. They asked me
how I'd come to interview with BEA, what I'd done before.
They mentioned my one appearance with City, and a woman
asked, —How is it you've never made it as a professional?

—Oh, I wasn't good enough, ma'am.

—Fair enough.

The manager said to me. —Say we took you on. If you were
with us for twenty years, what would your position be?

—I assume, sir, that by that time you'd know what a
wonderful person you had working for you, and would have
promoted me accordingly, to a position where my appearance,
honesty, and wonderful personality could be of use.

Every one of them burst out laughing.

—And if I've been working in the sky for twenty years, I understand one's heartbeat can be affected. Tremors.

(I do have a pacemaker today, actually, but I don't blame them.)

When it came to the end, they said there was nothing else to ask. I said, —If I may... When I was on the *Empire Pride* to Korea, I was with the Duke of Wellington's men, the Black Watch, the Green Howards. Some of them gave up their lives. And I remember being taught about tactics for withstanding interrogation, in case we were captured. This was obviously more important for the other regiments, than for me at my midget submarine base in Kure. But with all respects, I think I needed that training to endure what I've just gone through with you lot.

They burst out laughing again. I can hear it even now – that's a long time ago, isn't it? But I remember it like it was yesterday. It may seem strange, but at that moment, standing in the room with those people, I felt like it was the greatest achievement I'd ever had. A poor kid with no education...

—Thank you for the time, I said. I put my raincoat and trilby on *before* leaving, so they could see what I looked like before I came in. (It's called giving them a 'double front.')

I was so *elated*, having made the interview. I'd bluffed my way through, obviously. I left, started walking out through the airport – floating, really – passing the coffee tables. Then I heard this footstep behind me. —*Mr Holland!*

It was Mr Ellison, the manager – running through the airport.

—Yes sir?

—Sit down, he said. —I'm out of breath.

—I've not done anything wrong – there's nothing missing, is there?

—No! he said, breathing heavily. —You've got the job... We've never had an interview like you, Mr Holland. You've got a marvelous personality.

This is me: the kid with lice in his hair, rats in our home. I've brought a white handkerchief, and a black overcoat with a velvet collar because I wanted to look smart.

I wanted my dad to say, —*That's my son.* To give him something to be proud of.

BEA rented 'drop-off points' to save money on hotels and stuff, and in London I had to share an apartment with another steward, a lad from Glasgow. He was better educated than myself; most of the time I was just guessing. I knew I could do the bar work, of course, and a *bit* of numbers when needed. After each flight you had to square up the different currencies the passengers had used, take out for expenses, and total up the books. It all had to work out.

The Scotsman's name was Bill; he was with me at the beginning of my time at BEA, and still with me at the end.

For some reason I couldn't stay in the first place that BEA put me up. I phoned them up, and they moved me in with three other guys. There were two bunk beds in their apartment. So here I am, meeting the Welshman, the lad from Liverpool, and this very tidy, well-dressed gentleman.

I opened my suitcase to settle in, and would you believe: The Seven Veils, as neat as you please.

—Oooooohhh, I heard him say, I swear to you. He was in his element. I believe he actually shivered.

Now I had to phone the airport and figure out where *my* case had gotten to. With one thing and another they put me in contact with a woman who turned out to be a belly dancer.

Smashing!

No, it wasn't *smashing*. She gave me a right mouthful, as if I'd switched the cases on purpose! And I'd paid for transportation to the airport to make the second switch, and the nonsense of leaving these three men I'd just met...

I only had two pictures taken with BEA: one in my civilian clothes, with a stewardess, and one with a *different* belly dancer altogether, in Istanbul. I don't wish to give the impression that it was all belly dancers in those days. We also saw the natural wonders of the world: Gibraltar, for instance. I'd never seen so much stone in my life, the Rock of Gibraltar and all that. I always thought it was just a turn of phrase; they don't tell you it's an actual *rock*.

Our main 'schooling' as stewards was the emergency evacuation procedure: we were issued a very heavy axe, in case we needed to batter down a door. Very sophisticated.

I found the BEA steward examination difficult, though. They played something on a tape recorder, once, and expected you to respond, but I missed the beginning and couldn't make it out. When it came to us actually serving drinks and whatnot, I passed that with flying colours of course.

Well, they told me I hadn't passed the test – 'You've given some *ridiculous* answers,' they said, which was a bit personal if you ask me – but between the interview and Arthur Colbridge's recommendation, they moved me on.

(Lucky again.)

I looked smart in that double-breasted suit. Let's be honest: I've done harder jobs in my life than being an airplane steward.

Occasionally we faced some challenges, though.

At one point, two stewardesses and I were assigned to a big jetliner, 132 passengers. We got on the plane, and were told that a bomb had been planted on board – those were the days of IRA bombings, frightening stuff. My knees started giving way, I don't mind telling you. The captain said to the two stewardesses, — It's up to you. You don't have to work this flight if you don't want to.

The girls said they wanted to go!

I've been in plenty fights and been sent off to war, but this was more than I'd signed up for. What was I supposed to say, though? *I'd rather not, thanks?* I've never been a brave man, but I couldn't let those lunatics go and not join them.

Of course there was no bomb.

I say that working for BEA was a dream job: it let me travel, meet people, see the world in ways I'd never dreamt of before.

For instance, I was scheduled for a flight to Glasgow, and when we flew over Edinburgh, the captain flew low over the castle. It was a nice occasion for the passengers, but for me it was something special – I'd never seen anything like it; it was like seeing a different world. Thinking back on it now, it was a bit like going to Haifa when I worked on the airline, and seeing something so different from everything I'd known.

You get so many chances to realize how *small* the world is, and how *enormous* it is. It's all a matter of really seeing your surroundings.

Of course, when I got off the bus in Glasgow, one of the senior stewards came out. —Are you Holland?

—Yes sir.

—No going to work, we're on strike.

—I'm not in the union, sir.

—Well, you will be this afternoon.

Later on we went to Frankfurt. Lovely town. The senior steward was a chap called Bob Day, and...

I remember a very large banana...

I must tell you, I can't remember exactly what happened. Maybe that's best? I know that we had some fun with it, with a *very large banana*. There were two stewardesses there as well, and an overnight stay at a hotel.

Your guess is as good as mine.

The key to your room at this Frankfurt hotel was the biggest key in the world. Something like seven inches long, very beautiful. Again, this is in addition to the *very large banana*.

Mind you, if I remembered the trip, I might not be able to include it in this book. Maybe that's for the best.

Later on I had the honour of—

Or rather, Sir Peter O'Toole had the honour of meeting *me* on a flight to Paris.

I was the bar steward on this particular flight, and the stewardess came up and asked me, —Will you get me Peter O'Toole's autograph?

Now, I knew this man had made *Lawrence of Arabia*. I'd heard of him, I assumed he was an Irish fellow, but beyond that I had no idea who the man was.

—Wally, he's just over there.

He must have been an impressive man, judging from the way she was going on.

You must understand: there were *no* unattractive people on that entire flight. In those days, to be flying to Paris, you had money, you could afford to look smart, and everyone did. Including the stewards and stewardesses, I might add.

I had my tray, my silver dish full of dollar bills, my menu. I stopped next to the seat where she'd pointed: two, four, six, eight beautiful people without a care in the world. And there he was – I'd heard about his blue eyes and so forth. I leaned down and passed him a paper to sign inside the menu, *so as not to draw attention* to him, then stepped back to look around.

—What's this for? he asked.

I leaned back down. —Well, sir, I'm asking on behalf of the stewardess. (I didn't point to her in any way with my hand – *discreet*, you see.) She saw your *Lawrence of Arabia* and I gather she was very impressed.

I was conscious of not wanting to seem 'starstruck' – it's not as if I was a young boy, I was in my thirties. I think you would have been proud: I maintained dignity and composure even as he said, —Are you sure, good man? I'm a director at Barclay's bank.

A man was seated in the row directly behind him, with his wife, and I could see him mouthing some words, a message, which I realized went as follows: *I'm Peter O'Toole.*

I looked back, still holding onto the last bit of my dignity, to see the stewardess on her *knees* laughing.

He did sign the paper. No, not the bloody *banker*.

I handled George Harrison a bit more gracefully.

It was 1968; I was off duty at the time. He was flying with his wife Pattie Boyd. To talk to a movie star, someone from the city or from Hollywood, was one thing, but George Harrison was a lot younger, a Beatle from Liverpool – the lads who grew up on a Guinness and a jam butty. They're down-to-earth people in Liverpool. And whereas a young girl might be crazy to meet George, I was more interested in meeting his wife. (I was available, after all.)

So I approached Harrison with a bit more confidence: —Aye George, how are you lad?

It was like talking to one of the gang. And I think it was the same for him. The Beatles had never changed, you see. Well, except for one thing: he was wearing a bright pink safari suit.

Naturally I had to ask: —What're you doing in a *pink safari suit?* They'll think you're gay, George.

—Oh, I've got one in blue as well.

I told him I was glad he didn't wear them *together,* anyhow.

It really felt like talking to a kid the same as me. A millionaire kid, good luck to him, but he wasn't higher class, so to speak. Having said that, I wouldn't have walked up and said *By gum, yer lovely;* it was a nice flight, you have to adapt to your circumstances.

I did get to shake hands with Pattie Boyd, which was the highlight, really. I told her husband, —I quite like the suit, George; at your age you can get away with it.

Years later, in Puerto Rico with Cata, I bought two safari suits for myself – in blue *and* pink. Quite comfortable.

And I should tell you – though I don't like to brag, as you know – that I received from the airline a commendation for how I handled a particular passenger who'd committed manslaughter. Not on the plane, of course. He was being transported somewhere or other, and I saw that he was no disturbance.

I've had experience with the criminal element, as you'll recall.

This is how it ended:

We'd flown to Nice; I was the bar steward. The passengers had gone off, and the cleaner came up to me with two cartons of cigarettes, saying, —A passenger left these.

Two cartons of cigarettes were worth quite a few bucks, and I'd lost quite a bit of money on different flights. We used to have a silver bowl for putting our coins in, but I had a habit of putting my notes in there, and coins on top, to keep them all in one place. I'd had two £5 notes stolen not long before. It was my stupidity to leave them where they might be taken, I know. But when I was handed the cartons of cigarettes in Nice, I went and told the head steward on the flight, figuring the cigarettes would compensate me for the £10 I'd already lost. I think our wages were about £13 a week. I've still got a wage slip – in case I'm audited, I suppose.

So I said to the senior steward, —These will compensate me a bit for what I've lost.

He said it was up to me.

—Well, I've lost bleeding money, sir; they won't be bothered about a carton of cigarettes, will they.

I gave one carton to Bill Hickey, the senior steward back at the airport – who didn't know anything about where it came from.

My flatmate, Bill from Glasgow, was always shorter than me for money, and he smoked heavier than me as well. He asked if I had cigarettes, and I hadn't even opened the cartons yet. So I opened the second carton and gave him a packet, and put the rest away.

Time flies. Six weeks later, I was told to report to the head office, and was questioned. There was a letter asking whether I'd received two cartons of cigarettes and a bottle of whiskey. I said no to the latter, but yes, I'd received the cigarettes.

—What have you done with them?

—I gave one and a portion of the other away, I said, —but beyond that I've not touched them.

—You should have reported to the senior steward.

What was I going to say? That he was the one I'd given the carton to? The man had two children. He would have lost his job.

So I lost mine instead.

Do you know, I never had time to smoke any of the cigarettes.

Mr Ellison, the manager, was off when I lost my job. He came back the day I was leaving and said, —Mr Holland, you would not have lost your job if I'd been here. I'm so sorry to see you leave the company.

I broke down in tears to hear that. It meant a lot to me. I didn't dwell on it at the time, but it affected me, and stayed with me. I couldn't go back to Manchester to face the people I'd lived with all my life; I was too embarrassed.

So I took the first job I heard about, and finished up as a night porter in Newquay. I was lucky to have that work to fall back on, but for a while I was crushed. I felt I'd let everybody down, my dad most of all.

BEA fired Bill later on. I could have guided him a bit – he liked whiskey, which even I could have told him was no good. With a job like that, you've got to be on your toes, attentive to details.

In 1972, a BEA flight from Heathrow crashed near Staines. The plane stalled in the air and crashed. Everyone onboard died, more than a hundred people; it was the worst plane crash in British history. There was a senior steward on the plane, which was unusual.

If I'd been allowed to stay with the company, I suppose I'd have been senior steward by then.

I think about that sometimes. It seems like such a small thing, two cartons of cigarettes. But maybe it's not so small after all.

Chapter 13

Newquay again

After being dismissed from BEA, I went back to Cornwall, and worked as the night porter at the hotel facing the Minto. I couldn't bear to go home: I didn't want to face people. It's not that anybody knew, it was only Amy and Dad and my uncles and so forth, a few of the lads. But it was such a big thing to *get* the job, with no education. Where was I going to go, afterward?

I didn't want to disappoint my dad.

Telling him was the hardest thing.

Fortunately, it wasn't a bad situation in Cornwall. I made more money than anybody there – 'one of them things,' as they say. At the hotel, I was at the top of the village so to speak, so I could avoid meeting people. And I did do – as I say, I was the night porter, so I hid my face and spent some time alone.

In fact I didn't go into the village for a while – I was so conscious of it. The young people I worked with would go to the discotheque – this was 1968, 1969 – and invite me along. But at first I wouldn't go. The girls might be 18, the guys 22ish, maybe 25 – I was the oldest, at 31 years of age when I arrived.

And while everyone else there stayed young – working for a summer and then going off to the next thing, with another young person to take their place – I got a bit older every year.

So I was alone, at first.

It took me a *long* time to get over it—

—but it was the best thing that ever happened to me. If I hadn't gone back to Cornwall, I'd never have met the head bartender who pushed me to work at sea on the *Pendennis Castle*. I'd never have ended up on the 'Love Boat'...and I'd never have met Cata.

About the *Castle* (which we'll come to shortly): When I had my pacemaker put in, fifteen years ago – talk about a small world – the surgeon had been on the maiden voyage of the *Castle*. He told me all about it. Later he said the pacemaker wasn't working, and he would have to make arrangements to replace it on a Saturday. I asked him what arrangements he had to make, precisely? He said, —I've got to give up my golf this afternoon...

—Oh, I apologize for the inconvenience, I said.

—...and I'll put a new pacemaker in for your heart.

Well, if you insist!

That's fate, isn't it? You might say 'coincidence,' but I'm more than eighty years old, and these coincidences feel like fate to me.

I started to find my way back to life a bit.

The hotel's season finished up five weeks before the Minto. The hotel had only been open a couple of years, but the Minto was an older established place, with people coming back for twenty years. So with five weeks left before they closed for the winter, the Minto asked me to come over and take charge of the dining room, as maître d'; they even offered to pay me a bit extra, as they needed someone quickly. I'd have my own station, my own tables.

I got my own little place outside, overlooking the Gannel Estuary, and I was working with about five girls – it was great, actually. And I stayed for a few years, or rather, I came back every year for the tourist season.

It saved me, in a way. It put me in touch with people again.

There was another young man who'd come to the Minto, a quadriplegic boy. I had a collection of Japanese matchboxes – every establishment in Japan would give you these lovely matchboxes. Very beautiful, with different coloured heads on the matches. I gave him my collection of matchboxes, perhaps a hundred of them. His mother and father were thrilled to bits. And I was glad to give it to him: it meant so much to him, and he loved to look at it, and with the condition of his life, it was a chance to do something good. So I brought the matchboxes with me to Newquay at the beginning of the season, knowing he and his family would return.

I also gave him Alan Ladd's autograph, which I'd acquired during my brief but illustrious film career. I've never asked Alan whether he held on to *my* autograph; come to think of it, we haven't spoken since we worked together.

We had another customer named Maxie, a Londoner from Bow Bells (a Cockney) with a 'backward' son named Martin – I'll always remember him. A wonderful kid. I used to make a fuss of him at the table, and when I'd go down to the estuary, I'd offer to take Martin and his parents down. (His mum passed away during the few years that I was there.) Every year they'd come, every year they'd get the same table. Maxie wasn't a wealthy man, but a working man who'd done well, and he'd look after me a bit, moneywise. They were special people – they'd leave for London and write to me to let me know they'd arrived safely, that sort of thing.

There was one little girl that I'd helped as well, with her mother and father. She was eight or nine, from Yorkshire, and her mother told me, —She's so upset that she's leaving *you*, you know!

So I asked the little girl, —Will you write to me when you get home safely?

She did do...and I've always kept the letter. She wrote, *Thank you for looking after us.*

I get emotional thinking about it. It's nice in a way, getting emotional about things. I can move back and forth, in and out of the past, and have these deep feelings again – or for the first time.

Oddly enough, the little girl wrote in the same letter, *I saw Martin on the way home, and he waved.*

They'd passed each other on the drive back from Newquay. This was a child telling me about something that had happened to her on a journey. It was so...humane, like we were connected in a way I hadn't expected. They were just kids. Her mother and father wrote to me later as well: *We are so blessed. Thanks for all you did.*

I didn't do anything special. I was just glad to share a little bit of life with them, you see? Normal life. They wrote to the owner of the hotel as well, Tony Levinson, and I believe they mentioned me. Tony said to me after that first year, —You're coming back, aren't you? and when I did, they paid me even more money. I think they were glad to have me. Tony told me to come *before* the season started, to help get everything ready. I loved Cornwall, I was happy to do it. That gave me a chance to come down at my leisure with a place to stay, food every day, and I'd start preparing the dining room and so forth. I could get out into the village every night, watch TV downstairs in the hotel if need be.

In all the years since, I've never really thought about this, you know. I have grandchildren now, and arthritis, and after all it was only a job. It's not a story about traveling the world or meeting anyone famous. But it comes back to me now and I realize all over again how fortunate I was.

I'd arrive five weeks before the season started. Then the girls would come out, the waitresses and hostesses. Some would come year after year. There was one girl from Manchester, I used to call her 'Putty.' We got on fabulously. She was a marvelous waitress – I could rely on her 100%. You can't put a price on someone like that when you're working. And I liked and admired her as well.

We'd get the same crowd coming back year after year. The Levinsons, for instance: they had made some friends or acquaintances in Switzerland, and each year they'd take four Swiss girls to stay for the summer and learn a bit of English, and—

I've mentioned Smoky Bacon, haven't I?

Smoky gets his own section of the book.

Smoky

Eric Bacon, 'Smoky,' was my best pal. He lived near me in Manchester; we were close pals as teenagers, and went into the army together. Here's the sort of man Smoky was: one time, we bumped into a crowd from Liverpool at a dance hall, and this guy picked on me. Smoky came over – he was quite a big lad – and said, —Hey, if you want to fight, fight *me*.

Well, Smoky beat the guy. But he put himself in danger because he was my friend, and he was willing to do it to save me that trouble.

When we were in the Army, he was in Trieste and I was in Korea and Japan. He was demobbed a month before me (he's a month older than me). He wrote to me about Elvis, and odd lapels. Everything seeming new.

I wrote back to him: *No, no, that won't affect me, Smoky. I won't be changing like you.*

(But I did change.)

We played for the same soccer team – Smoky was center-half. He was a *smashing* player, better than me. I think back on it now, and he could have been a professional, if he'd stopped smoking.

Smoky was adopted, which was something unusual for our time. At least it seemed that way. They were rough and tumble people, working class. Smoky's mother and father owned a shop – he could always get cigarettes. He never stopped smoking. Fortunately, I did, the day my eldest son was born.

Smoky married a beautiful Irish girl named Violet. I was his best man, of course, and godfather to their daughter. About five guys on the soccer team had wanted to ask Violet for a date, but she and Smoky clicked – they were happy together. A few years ago, I got in touch with her. And she told me when I called, — You were the only one on the team who never asked me for a date! Why was that? I really liked you!

—Well, you were going with my best pal. It's just not done.

I'm quite old-fashioned in that way. (Not in every way, I admit.)

I have other stories about Smoky, but I've decided to play them close to the vest, so to speak.

Smoky's children are grown now, of course. His first son became a detective in Manchester. And Smoky's daughter, my goddaughter, became a stewardess. All this I've only learned in the last few years.

Smoky didn't get as far away from it as I did, so to speak. But then, I was lucky. I was a roamer.

From then on I went back to Newquay at the beginning of the season, and at season's end I'd stay a week to tidy up and such. Besides our good wages, the owner of the Minto – Tony Leverton his name was – would always give us a bonus. He looked after me very well. His mother and fatherwere quite old – in their 70s, which doesn't seem so old anymore, I suppose – and his mum never believed me when I told her the things I'd done. Working for BEA, in the army, all that. —Oh, you're such a liar, she'd say.

I'd laugh with her about it, but it pissed me off.

I've never been a liar. There's no *need*, is there, especially when you've lived a life like mine.

In those days I also worked at Stirk House, in the countryside outside of Clitheroe. It was similar to what you'd see on *Downton Abbey*. Old money, and in England 'old' means something. I knew the area well: during the evacuation, Grandma would take us to Clitheroe on a Saturday, maybe with Dickie and Kathleen, the next door neighbours. There was a cake shop where they made beautiful bread, and Grandma would buy the things we needed for the week. Then Grandma would make bread for everybody on the row.

The village where Stirk House was located was named Gisbourne. Remember Robin Hood? Sir Guy of...well, there you are.

The fellow who owned Stirk House was a big man, a sharp dresser, and always very nice to me. Luigi – an Italian, believe it or not – was the main bartender, very experienced and far superior to *me* at the job. I learned a lot from him, though one night he got a bit cheeky and I nearly killed him...which doesn't mean he wasn't a marvelous bartender.

At Stirk House I used to have to wear an evening suit all day – the local fox hunt would come in, and I'd have to serve hot toddies on a silver tray.

The headwaiter and his pal used to knock about with two girls named Anne and Maureen – both very beautiful, would dress like millionaires. They were part of the Piccadilly crowd, the Chez Joey crowd. They were secretaries with good educations, making a lot of money, and guys flocked to them. I knew Maureen's sister Cathy, who went out with a pal of mine.

One year, I'd just come back from Cornwall, and I took Maureen out for a bit. I didn't have much money but I had to dress nicely when I went out with her, with her fox stole around her neck. Everybody we'd see would just stare at her. She was like a movie star. Well, one thing led to another – things tend to do that – and she married Peter King, who'd pulled me out of the river at Stonyhurst and saved my life.

Anne, the other girl, was working in Newark, New Jersey. She was going out with the D.A., with money to prove it. She and her boyfriend were going to marry, but he died of cancer – a shocking death – and on the rebound, so to speak, the ended up with the D.A. She got a marvelous job working for him as well. (I'm not sure whether she got the job or the D.A. first.)

A few years later, on a strip to Stonyhurst, I called in at Stirk House with Zena, who'd been my girlfriend when I first went to Cornwall. It had been renovated, and I couldn't recognize the place at all.

You turn your back for a minute and the past disappears. Still, it was a nice feeling to see the place though I couldn't remember everything.

Zena ended up marrying a man named Bob Kenyon, but we've always stayed in touch. A few years ago they even came to Ellicottville to visit.

Zena's the one person I know who might have seen more of the world than me, besides my dear friend, the astronaut Buzz Aldrin.[5] A few years ago Zena needed surgery, and a mistake was made. As compensation she got a certain amount of money, which wasn't a lot compared to what you get in America, but it lets them travel and see the world. Even Ellicottville. I can't blame them.

Sue Kennedy was an Australian woman, about 26 years old when I knew her. She was a con merchant. I was the bar manager at the Bristol, where they wouldn't even let the Beatles and Stones stay. Sue came into the bar. Now, during the day I'd wait tables and let someone else handle the bar, because I could make more money at the tables. Sue would come in – she was working as a hostess at a hotel – and she was *stunning*. I thought, My God, I'd like to share some sandwiches with her. (I may be paraphrasing.) She came in with this good-looking guy – *c'est la vie* – but the next time she turned up she was with an different fellow, older. Hmm.

I asked her for a date one time, and we went out. I realized pretty quickly she was trying to con me: she started talking about ordering champagne. —Champagne? You must be joking, love.

And she admitted it: —Yeah, I take guys for suckers.

It's a living, I suppose. But that wasn't for me. —Well, take me off your list.

---

[5] (My dear friend Buzz Aldrin met me once.)

But I liked her. We carried on for a while, afterward, since we both knew where we stood. And she sent a letter to her mother and father: 'If Wally ever comes to (whatever town she was from), give him whatever he needs, he's a great guy,' and so forth. She lived in Queensland, in Australia.

You may recall that I've had some experience with Australians, though, and I have never been tempted to make the trip.

The headwaiter at Stirk House had worked on the QE2. We'd get a night off, and would go to a smashing place in Blackburn. (In Gisbourne, a night in Blackburn was like going to the big city.)

We made decent money at the hotel. I lived in – I got my food and a place to stay, and didn't need to be anywhere else. The chap who owned the place, a big builder named Jack, was the image of Alan Hale, 'Little John' from *Robin Hood*. Luigi and I would work together on the same bar; if there was a wedding, I'd go to the second bar by the dancefloor. A beautiful place.

I had no idea we were so close to Clitheroe. I've told you before I'm useless with directions. One of us always had a car, especially the headwaiter, and you know how it is in cars – you don't always notice what's around you.

There was a wedding at Stirk House once in 1969, and the bride's father was a cattle merchant – in charge of all the meat in Lancashire, basically. There were *two* bands, one playing rock'n'roll, one playing softer music. Most people make do with one, don't they? Outside, two long tables. I remember them absolutely *cluttered* with presents – thousands of pounds' worth.

I remember at the time a gold lighter called 'Ronson,' an expensive item. There were *seven* of them on the table. (Again, one is usually enough, isn't it?) I've never seen so many envelopes full of money in my life, either, but the best was yet to come.

At midnight, the French doors at the side of the dancefloor opened, and a red Spitfire automobile drove in. Maybe it was a gift for the bride and groom, though there's always a chance the driver just made a wrong turn.

On my day off I'd go to the racetrack.

The headwaiter lived in Manchester as well, so I could take a bus to meet him and we'd drive out to Gisbourne. And I could go home for a couple of days to see Dad.

Anyhow, one winter day he and I been out somewhere and were driving back. There was a lot of ice, black ice. We were on a local road parallel to the motorway, in his big old-fashioned Austin car. I said to him at one point, —Oh my God, I thought we were going to crash there.

At that very moment he turned around the bend, and the car turned over on its side.

I was in a good suit and my best overcoat, with a velvet collar. He was similarly dressed. Now the car's on its side, and he's directly above me in his seat, and I'm on the bottom, by the ground, strapped in.

He stood on *top* of me to open the door, which was up instead of to the side for a change. And he called down to me, —Get out quick, Wally! *The petrol's leaking.*

I jumped out like lightning. It's a miracle I didn't set the petrol on fire myself.

We were both injured in the same place – the side of the knee and the right elbow. We were more shaken than hurt, honestly. The overcoat got it worse, with the headwaiter stepping on it. I didn't step on *his* overcoat, I'd point out.

I do wonder if we'd have crashed if I hadn't said anything.

At any rate, I say I've been quite lucky in my life, and if the choice is a ruined overcoat or being stuck in a burning car leaking petrol, I suppose I can always buy a new coat.

CHAPTER 14

The real 'love boat'

Remember the old series, *The Love Boat?* It was no comparison to the real thing.

In the late 1970s and early 80s I lived and worked in the Caribbean, which suited me – you can wear white linen trousers all year without looking like a fool. How did I get there? By way of South Africa, as you do.

In 1974 I took a job as a steward on the passenger liner *Pendennis Castle,* on an eleven-day route between Southampton and Cape Town, South Africa. The head bartender used to come to the Minto, and recommended it. I met this young guy – well, 'young,' I was in my thirties and he was only twenty. A smashing guy – we became friends. A friend of his joined him, so the three of us worked on the cruise line together. The job itself wasn't much to speak of, honestly – the *Pendennis Castle* used to carry the post back and forth, and was never luxurious like the 'Love Boat.' Still, it got more sun than Newquay, and after working for BEA and coming back to Cornwall I wanted to get out, see the world again.

I did say I was a roamer – and a lucky man.

At sea, traveling abroad, I'd find myself in situations I'd never see in England. For instance, in Cape Town I founded a riding school on the side. Well, not really: I 'founded a riding school,' meaning I organized the guys from the ship to go riding. It was a side job – I was on my toes, being nippy, making a couple of bucks. It didn't cost me anything, and besides that, it used to be great fun.

You've got to make a buck, as they say in America. One way or the other, you've got to make enough to get by. What that means is, when a chance comes by, you *must* take it. I've never understood people who don't live that way.

Anyhow, five or six of us used to go regularly; our little riding school became quite popular. On one occasion, twelve of us drove out to the stables. Of course, we didn't have twelve horses. So six of us went out first, then the next six when we returned. One of the lads had been an apprentice jockey, so he knew how to ride – far better than me. I always just pretended I could ride. Nobody showed me how, I just got on and dug in.

Life is like that, in my experience.

Well, the six of us went out, enjoyed it, came back, and the other five made their way back to the ship. The next six set out riding, and I said I'd wait for them at the stable. So I went to sleep in a hammock. Perhaps you see where this is heading.

I woke up, everyone had gone, and now I was a bit frightened: I had to get back to the ship, but I was in a stable in the wilderness in South Africa with no transportation.

Now, a lot of wealthy people had horses there. The Defense Minister of South Africa stabled two horses there. So I made my way to the bottom of the trail and waited outside. And a few minutes later, a Rover came down the pathway. A beautiful car. I jumped in front of the car and said, —Excuse me sir! I'm in a bit of a desperate situation here. If I don't get back to the ship, I'll lose my job...

The man looked at me for a moment and said, —You're from the north of England, aren't you?

—Yes I am. Where are you from?

—I'm from Blackpool.

Halfway around the world and I meet a man from *Blackpool,* less than an hour from Hurst Green. I'd even worked at one of the posh hotels in Blackpool during winters when I was back from Newquay. (And while I'm telling you about it: the chap who'd won the biggest amount of money ever on the Pools, £300,000 – that was a big win in the Sixties – I'd served him there at the hotel, at my table. A mean bastard he was, from Birmingham.

Don't know why I've told you that.)

—Blackpool? Great, I've worked there. What do you do here?

—I have a couple of horses here.

It was like I was talking to one of my mates. If I find that I'm talking to someone speaking in a refined way, I'll conduct myself that way. But if they're down to earth like me, I'll be down to earth.

—Blimey. Two horses? You must have a good job.

—Well, I've retired.

—You're so young! (He was late forties, fifty at most.)

—What kind of work did you do?

—I worked for Lloyd's of London. I was a millwright, doing the engineering under the bottom of ships.

I didn't realize that was the kind of job where you retired by age fifty. Well, then he said, —There were five of us, and we discovered gold bullion.

—You *what?*

—So I was a millionaire overnight.

—Bleeding hell.

I've still got his business card.

That reminds me: Africa's the place for that sort of meeting. When I was onboard ship, one of the officers was reading Wilbur Smith's latest book, and left it on a chair. And when they came back I'd picked it up and returned it, saying, —Oddly enough, he's my favourite writer. (I wasn't just saying that either; Wilbur Smith did *Shout at the Devil* and *Gold Mine*, made into movies with Roger Moore, if I remember rightly.)

The officer said, —Oh, I met him. In Johannesburg. Walked into the office, and he worked for the income tax people, the government. He had his feet on the table, and apologized to me. I told him it didn't bother me. He says: 'I've just become a millionaire overnight. My book's sold a million copies.'

I wouldn't say I've 'lived history' or anything like that, that's just silly. But you might say, every once in a while you feel it brush by your shoulder. You realize how near it always is.

I lived with Nobby and Colin in those days in Charlton, in a modern apartment near Bob and George – at some point, I think everyone lives with someone named 'Nobby,' don't they. I moved in with them the first year I came back from Cornwall, and kept coming back.

Nobby's real name was Norman. He was a character – 6'2", handsome bastard he was. Women would *drool* over him, and he certainly didn't mind. He'd left his wife and kids when I met him, but he took care of them. It wasn't for me to question him. In later years he went back to her, when their children were a bit older, and his son became one of the top stunt pilots in England, flying jets in formation. Nobby was thrilled, as you'd imagine.

Our apartment was very luxurious – I can't remember if I had my own bed or not, but I was grateful to be able to stay with them.

I'd come back from Africa after eleven days with a fabulous suntan, even in winter. We'd go to parties, or a place out in the countryside, and 'make the scene,' so to speak – and that suntan would give me a bit of an edge. Which I needed, around Nobby. (It doesn't take much to have a better tan than an Englishman.)

I used to get the best cigars and cologne cheap, in Africa, so I could sell them when I got back. (Let's not quibble about legality at this point.) Nobby and Colin mended televisions, making decent money, so we let it be known that ours was the apartment where the parties would happen of a weekend.

Nobby loved telling women I worked on the *Queen Elizabeth,* which somehow reflected well on *him.* —Oh, Wally goes to *Africa.*

Well, the girls certainly liked talking to him, anyway.

Nobby and I were making a few bucks, and I'd come home on leave with a bottle of Bacardi, cigars, nice aftershave. It was a style. Of course all this camaraderie all only went so far: I left some money under a cushion or something, once, and Nobby and Colin knew where it was. —Well, Wally, we borrowed a few quid while you was away.

Good people, all the same.

Colin's the brother of George's wife and Bob's wife. Everyone used to call him 'The Cincinnati Fireball,' after a hit number that he used to sing quite well. Of course, George would do his Sinatra tunes. At parties, they'd both perform – we were always out laughing, drinking, singing, and then I'd be away for weeks in Africa, the Caribbean, flying to Switzerland with five girls... I can't believe it myself, looking back. What I mean is, I can't believe I was able to come so far from one life to another, and then another, and then...

Did I tell you we went to Lake Geneva with five girls? Well, I'm telling you now. It's my memoir, so I can tell you twice if I like.

I can't remember their names or what the hell we did in Switzerland, but I probably wouldn't tell you if I could. They were all very bright, educated. One of them had come to Newquay on vacation, where we met, and I arranged to go to her house on the lake. She brought a few friends, so did I.

It gets cold in Switzerland, so I borrowed an overcoat – and not 'borrowed' in the sense Nobby and Colin 'borrowed a few quid' while I was away, either.

That's all for that story: Switzerland, and I borrowed an overcoat. This is what my son Wally calls an 'anticlimax.' You get those sometimes in life.

I've not seen Nobby for years. I don't even how to reach him anymore. When I say 'It's a different world,' that's one thing I mean.

The head bartender and I heard that they needed staff on the *Queen Elizabeth*, which was going on a world tour, so to speak. On the *Pendennis Castle* you'd only go away for eleven days at a time, so this was an adventure indeed.

They put me in the first-class dining room. I didn't have that much experience at that level of quality. What I'd done in the holiday seasons, anybody with good manners could get by; there you were dealing with a mix of working-class people and others who've got a few bob and *think* they're not working-class. This was something else, the haves rather than the have-nots.

It was wonderful but a bit uncomfortable, in a way. I'd never acted at that time, on the stage, except for my comedic turn with the dancer's bosom. I was exceptionally shy, as I had been all my life, being so small as a boy.

(I remember the girls at Calico Printers would ruffle my hair, tease me. And I was always embarrassed, but the attention...)

On the *QE2* I felt like I was in a new world. The first-class passengers came from all over, but were mostly Americans. They'd come on for a week or ten days, and would leave envelopes at the end of the week, for our service. We made decent money, but we earned it: each of two waiters would serve sixteen people in the first-class service. Orders went in separately from the other dining rooms, separated out before they even reached the kitchen. I was fast on my feet, and had good teachers – the chap I was working with, a tubby Spanish fellow, was a marvelous waiter.

I'd handle first-class service if they needed me, then alternate with two other lads in…'tourist' class, you might say. That's where you found everyone else – the people like me, who might just go on one cruise in their lives.

And I'd see to the entertainers.

I keep emphasizing the word 'lucky,' and I will again, just now: on the QE2, we had an 'extension' room where we'd put the entertainers. They earned good money, full accommodations, but not *fabulous* exactly. Oddly enough, there was one comedian, a chap named Tony Crawley, whom I'd met years earlier in Cornwall…

The Mersey Hotel in Cornwall, 300 yards from where I'd lived, was owned by a professional rugby player for Wigan. He'd come to the house that day and said, —The employment bureau tell me you're an out-of-work bartender.

—Well, I'm out of work because I *want* to be – I've just come back from working away.

Have I already told this story? Anyhow I'm telling you now.

—I need to hire somebody, said the rugby player.

—I wish you good luck, I told him.

—No no, I need you badly. I'll pay you good money.

He did say *'good money,'* so you can see where this is going: one thing led to another, and I took the job. Only having to walk 300 yards to work was ideal. I was in charge of the lounge during the day. The Mersey had the top people in Britain performing on weekends at the cabaret. And Tony Crawley would come through and perform.

I wouldn't see the performances; I was in the bar all day, and didn't work nights. One day a customer came in and said, —I want you to know how much I enjoyed your show. I thought you were *great.*

I looked around. —Who are you talking to? I asked.

—*You!* said the customer. He seemed terribly excited to see me. —You're Tony Crawley, aren't you?

I'd never laid eyes on the man. I'd heard of him, of course.

—You're the bloody image of him, he said. —Black curly hair and dark glasses.

I'm not Tony Crawley, that I know of.

At any rate, here we are in tourist class, and I heard that Tony Crawley was playing onboard the ship. Still hadn't ever seen him. And it wasn't as if we could just walk up and see the performances – this wasn't the *Countess;* no, on the QE2 we followed protocol. So I still had no idea what he looked like. But I'm at the bar and I see this Irishman coming down. He sees me at the bar, and calls out: —Are you Wally Holland?

—Yes sir! You Tony Crawley?

(I never did get a picture of him, but there's no need – just flip to one of the pictures of me in this book, and squint. Handsome man, obviously.)

And now it's years later and I move to the *Countess.* Naturally, Tony Crawley joins up as the resident comedian. And naturally, we became quite good friends.

I think the word is *kismet...?* If not, it should be.

Kismet works both ways though. While I was on the *QE2* I missed going to Russia by only two days, because I was on vacation. (I've never been since.)

There were four of us sharing a cabin. We used to have a drinking contest with Bacardi and Coke. It was a 12x8 cabin, give or take, two bunks on either side, and a stool to sit on; we'd all crowd in for this contest. Each of the other fellows was in his twenties. It was Stuart Rowberry and the other two (pals of his), all of us drinking. They'd smoke pot as well, which was fine – I've never touched it in my life.

The stakes in the contest were £5. Well, we only made £13 a week, so with three of them playing, I stood to gain a week's wages...

I'd tell jokes, someone would say something foolish. We'd watch blue movies sometimes. And I'd drink half my cocktail and throw away the other half in the disposal bin...

Yes, of *course* I cheated. The napkins in the bin would soak it up, I'd tie up the bag, they'd never cotton on to me.

This is part of the education that Unkie and my dad gave me, you see.

So we had this competition: who would last the longest before falling asleep or getting intoxicated? And I'd always win. Fifteen quid each time!

Maybe that's why we only played twice.

Another time, I'd been to the bookies on the Saturday and backed two winners. If I'm not mistaken, I won £21, far more than a week's wages, but I couldn't collect the money right away – we were on a New York cruise from England, eleven days at sea. And all of a sudden my wallet went missing. I reported it, but what can you do?

Now, a Scottish lad was sharing my cabin at the time, and he'd stolen it. I only found out by luck: without my wallet I couldn't collect the bet, could I. But I went to the bookies and tried anyway: —I remember the horses I backed, but I've not got my ticket as my wallet was stolen, etc.

Of course this never works. But they remembered: —Oh, we paid it out. Must've been the person who stole your ticket, he said. The chap knew him: —I've got an idea of him... He's...*Scottish.*

I felt like a detective after that. I can't remember whether I got the money or the wallet back. I do remember he was a creeping bastard, though.

In 1976, a Cuban airline crashed off the coast of Barbados.

At the time, me and my mate Knockout were on the beach with two women off the ship. (Knockout was always saying to people: 'I'll knock you out!' I can't be sure, but I suspect it wasn't his *given* name.)

Anyhow, the plane had crashed down quite near to the ship. Everyone aboard was killed. The lads on duty on the ship had to go out and bring the bodies in from the sea. At the same time, there was an Irish woman arrested – talks of sabotage. We saw them take her away. It was a group of Cubans who did it, though, and I read recently that the American government knew about it.

I didn't mind being far away from history, so to speak, that time. Honestly I can't remember the beach today, what it looked like, or my mate or the two women. I remember there was *some* beach. But if you'd told me I was halfway around the world that day I'd've believed you. That's how it is, and you can be grateful for the things that pass you by as much as the things that happen to you.

In summer 1976 I volunteered to join the Cunard *Countess*, cousin to the *Princess*. The *Princess* was more popular, or visible – Grace Kelly launched that ship, and Neil Armstrong's wife launched the *Countess*.

The *Countess* was a brand new ship registered in England, built in Denmark, furnished in Italy, and based in Puerto Rico. We had to be in Italy for two months, living onboard ship, while the *Countess* was being furnished. We lived as best we could – we only worked until 5:00 every day, then we pissed off for the night. It was our regular pay, and lodgings weren't great but they were free. (The unions made sure we were taken care of.)

The *wine* was cheap, though, and it was Italy in summer – say no more.

It was like two months' vacation, like being in a movie.

I'm no expert, but I'd venture to guess that 72% of the crew was gay men, which worked to *my* advantage in terms of meeting women. Years later, of a weekend I'd bring a bunch of the guys home to meet Cata, have a Saturday dinner. She loved them – a nice crowd.

Anyhow, that's how I moved from the *Queen Elizabeth* to the real 'Love Boat.' I'd work three months every day, possibly twelve hours a day, and then I'd get a month's paid vacation, and Cunard would fly me to wherever I needed to go.

Now, being single and with the aforementioned black curly hair, I had *several* places to go, by which I mean: invitations from passengers to come visit. I'd spend a week with one, a week with another, and so on. A law professor in Miami, very intelligent; a Canadian divorcée; and so on.

Needless to say, I hadn't met my wife at this point. This isn't that sort of story; I'm not that sort of person.

They tended to be older women, of course – five to ten years older than me. Some of them were divorced or married, which is one reason I don't go into details. The other reason is old-fashioned, in a way: it's just not done. That was another way of life altogether, and I enjoyed it, but it hasn't been my life since I met Cata. Younger people might not understand this: *I've never missed it.*

I used to tend bar for the ship's captain, in his private cabin. I'd be working in the casino, the lounge, the discotheque, or on deck. We'd alternate, month to month. Being on deck was the main thing: on the open deck, you'd see a lot of beautiful women hoping to enjoy themselves on vacation, no worries. I'll never again see beauty like that – women from all over the world, Irish, Danish, African. In Newquay you were surrounded by young people working for the summer, which was lively and fun. On the ship, though, it was often older women, divorced, separated, of thinking about getting married – different reasons you'd go on vacation.

I met Miss Universe once in Puerto Rico, but she was nothing compared with some of these women on the ship. Being at sea, on the beach, being catered to with nothing to worry about – it brings out something inside a person. They glow.

Now, the captain, Peter, would come to the deck with the Purser. The captain knew how to take care of the guests. There was a particular woman, 35 years old or so with an eight-year-old daughter; the captain would say, —Wally, take a piña colada over to that woman.

—And one from me please, said the Purser.

Now, Colonel Coombs[6] was sat in the chair, and he said, —By the way, Wally, would you ask that lady if she'd like to have a drink? And he pointed to the same lady.

I had to be diplomatic. —Colonel, I said, —When you're in your Bermuda shorts, these women don't realize that you are in fact a colonel, or a man of status, or a very wealthy man. It doesn't exactly *show*, sir. Here, you're just somebody in shorts.

—Wally, *what* are you implying?

—What I am suggesting, sir, is that you've got a roving eye – nothing wrong with that, you're a widower – but that's the most beautiful and sensuous woman *I've ever* seen, and I'm inclined to think the captain and purser agree with me, as they've sent drinks over accordingly.

He seemed resigned. —Alright, Wally.

—I'll do my best for you all the same, sir.

She did take a drink off him, though. Why not? He was paying. I wouldn't know if they met.

I was doing the captain's parties at the time. Guests would come onboard of a Saturday, free lunch and drinks. And Sunday was a special captain's party, where all the stewards and captain would meet every passenger on the ship in the lounge, shake hands, and so forth.

Of a Monday, the captain would have a *private* party for VIPs. Well, money buys you that. But the captain could also invite whomever he liked. Like this woman, for instance.

Colonel Coombs had this business card in his wallet: 'Retired colonel, wife left me penniless,' that sort of thing – respectfully making his situation clear to whomever he might meet on the ship. To save time, you might say, and avoid uncertainty.

---

[6] (I know he sounds like a TV character, but he was an actual ex-colonel by the name of Coombs)

I've got a similar card these days, I don't mind telling you. It's best to be up front about things. Everybody laughs when they see it, which is all it's meant to do. But the colonel's card had to serve double duty, so to speak; he wasn't always after a laugh...

I was in the captain's cabin when Peter Ustinov turned up at the party, and (separately) the Prime Minister of Grenada, Mr Gairy, just prior to him being overthrown. I know that the captain invited Sir Peter to make a speech – he could speak Spanish, French, Russian, English. A marvelous intellect, and it was a privilege to hear.

The ship is like a world of its own, and then there's a smaller world inside, which you had to be invited in to. I was *lucky* to be invited.

On one occasion the captain came on deck and said to me, — You know Wally, you should be paying Cunard to let you work here.

I felt that way sometimes.

First thing in the morning, while most everyone was asleep and the staff were cleaning the ship, the captain would go by himself to play the piano in the casino. I came across him doing that once – I'd been up all night for one reason or another, and was passing through on the way to my cabin, and heard Peter playing. It was lovely and surprising; I stood there in amazement. When he saw me, he put his fingers over his lips, meaning: never to discuss what I'd seen. It was something he could keep secret. I suppose that was important, on such a crowded ship.

They got good reports about me from passengers. Well, I worked like a dog. Later on, when I got married, Cunard allowed me to leave the *Countess* and come back – a nice compliment. I got a wonderful letter of support from Lt Collinson.

One time on deck, I'd gotten an ice cream, which wasn't quite correct – we weren't supposed to have any, but it's not the end of the world, is it. The captain came down at the same time. I ducked out of the way. He pointed at me: —I saw you, Wally. I saw you!

But of course it was no trouble. We were in it together – men and women, passengers and crew and officers. Everything about the experience was meant to be beautiful, and fun.

––––––––––––––––

This was the 1970s, mind you. Today it's a different world. But you live in the world you live in. I had learned the right way of approaching people: respectful, polite. —Good *morning* sir, good day madam, how *are* you.

They used to call me 'Mr Shoehorn' – I was easy to get on with. I'd see a beautiful woman putting on suntan lotion and offer to help: —Madam, for $5 you don't have to do that yourself.

—I don't believe in paying for this, she'd say.

—Oh no Ma'am, I'd pay *you!*

It went over very well. No harm done either way, of course. That was the important thing.

I always had a lot of jokes in my back pocket, and could ad-lib a bit. You are what you are, and also what you decide to make yourself into. And I *did* try to be something I wasn't. I was tremendously shy as a young boy, couldn't even walk across the dance floor to ask a girl to dance. If she said no, to have to walk all the way back afterward... But if you can approach someone with respect, and with a bit of *fun*, then you can make it a different sort of conversation altogether. A bit of fantasy.

On each voyage you had a choice of islands to go ashore: Barbados, St Thomas – and whereas you couldn't be personal in your conversations aboard ship, if you met a passenger on shore, you could converse in a different way. Of course, the crew could invite passengers to the crew bar, below decks...and the officers could invite passengers to *their* bar.

So you had a rivalry – and a lot of jealousy, by the way. Sometimes you'd have a woman invited the first night by an officer, finding out that her friend was drinking with the crew. I got into a confrontation with an officer about that once, over some petty jealousy. He tried to take a liberty with me, and we nearly got into a fight.

I just avoided getting sacked that time: the union stepped in and handled my case. He said I'd attacked him 'verbally and viciously.' Which I did, to be fair; I told him to fuck off. But I managed to keep my job, even though one of the officers senior to him, a jealous bastard, tried to get me off the ship. It worked out alright in the end.

But that's part of life, jealousy. And in my position, you could understand it. I was on top of the world.

This is what my eldest son calls a 'brief digression':

There was a lovely woman from Eastern Airlines, whom I had a brief affair with. She's the one who told me, —Don't *ever* go to Chicago.

And I never did, until I went to my son's graduation there, and I was so surprised – it's one of the most beautiful cities I've ever been to! It's not Paris or Vienna or Tokyo, the *older* places. But Chicago is lovely. Worst advice I ever got – I should have ignored that stewardess altogether. They're always getting me into trouble.

On the *Countess*, we had two chaps called Stringfellow and Tuttle – they were a couple. Tommy Stringfellow was in charge of the union. The *Countess* was built prior to her sister ship, the

Princess, which only went to a handful of ports. We went to Venezuela, Grenada, Barbados, Martinique, St Thomas, and Puerto Rico – a different port every day.

On the *Countess*, we'd work for a month at a time. Freddy Cochran had been at sea for thirty-five years or more. He'd worked on the *Mauretania* – not the one that was decommissioned before I was born, the other one. And not the one that was sunk with the torpedo either: that was the *Lusitania,* which was before my time, if you can imagine.

We had a strike onboard ship in October 1980. The company was talking about selling the ships, and they planned to register in the Bahamas and hire foreign crew, who weren't union members. It was the second time there'd been trouble with the crew, and they revolted — there was a strike. Cunard ended up *firing* the entire crew, but they took them back in the end.

There was some uneasiness going around the crew. The unions were talking about stopping the ship doing its course. It wasn't profitable or some such thing. Cunard wanted to get rid of the unions, of course. Tommy Stringfellow was going on vacation with Mr Tuttle, and he asked me, —Wally, could you stand in for me as union man? As you've been in the union before.

I had indeed, as a kid – but only as a listener, not a speaker.

I honestly can't imagine myself speaking for the union, or where it might have happened. I don't just mean that I can't remember it, but given what I know of myself, it seems *impossible* that I got up at a meeting to speak on behalf of the union. But I did. I went into the meeting and said basically this to the company representatives:

—Sir, you can't compare the *Princess* and our ship. You wonder where the profits are. Well, in terms of expenses, in the lounge, the service hatch is at the back of the room; there's a mistake been made there by the builders of the ship. There's an exit door with thousands of volts of electricity, and a swimming pool upstairs with tiles coming off. There's a bar in the center of the top deck that's never been used in the months we've been at sea, and problems with the toilets – there's *excreta* coming up from the pipes, and I can tell you why. We're in port every day, and people going ashore first thing and coming back around dinner wanting a shit and a shower. The discotheque's air conditioning is breaking down because it's packed. The ship isn't losing because of *us*, but because of the way it was built. You're blaming the crew for nothing. So please don't compare our ship to the other.

For some reason it was found agreeable, and that was that.

Well done, eh?

What do you mean 'well done,' I was *pissed out of my head*. I had to have a drink, otherwise I was too shy. And why not? Sometimes you need a glass of wine to get ready for church. Sometimes you're going on stage in a play and you add a bit of wine to your Gatorade.

The important thing is to be prepared.

Teddy Cochran didn't agree with the strike. The *Princess* was in Puerto Rico then, and the union asked me to let them know what was going on with the *Countess*. I was known as 'our man in Puerto Rico.' The bar stewards were in a special group of their own, a sort of clique. The main bar steward was a big Londoner, married but always chasing women. And they threw him off the ship – he was a union man, but they got rid of him.

He ended up getting a job with the Norwegian line, I believe, as a head bartender.

In those days, when you docked in St Thomas, you could get a bottle of Dom Perignon for $10 or so, a bottle of gin for a dollar. Now, out of a bottle of gin you get 32 shots of liquor. Imagine running three bars, packed to the gills, and putting a bottle of your own gin in with what the ship is supplying – you could do $1,000 a week without anyone knowing, and your wages on top of that. The union men didn't like that, as you'd imagine. The wine stewards had something going as well: you could put cheap wine in an expensive bottle, and none of the guests would know the difference.

On the *Queen Elizabeth*, one of the top bartenders had left the company, retired, and the income tax people went after him and charged him thousands of pounds. But just imagine what he'd made over the years! In those days it wasn't easy to keep track of such things or investigate, on the ship. So prior to the bartender being sent down the gangway, Cunard had people sit at each end of the bar, pal around with the guests and the bartenders, to check on the employees, keeping track of what went into the till. Then they'd confront the workers about it.

The union didn't like that, as you'd imagine. Well, who would?

Teddy Cochran had been a union man most of his life, but he didn't agree with them in the end. And it's amazing how many of his friends turned against him. As I say, when you get money and politics together, that's how things are.

Teddy was a small man, old – a smashing fellow. He'd have a go with anyone same as me, if they wanted to fight. He adored his wife, and used to say he couldn't understand how she married him. (I couldn't either.)

Years later, his son wrote to me to say he'd died of cancer.

There aren't many of us left, you know.

Working on the *Countess* was one of the best times of my life. I've been on a few cruises since then, and it's certainly easier when you don't have to work, but I look back on it and I'm so grateful. That's a nice feeling: to be able to look at five or ten years of your life and have no regrets, just gratitude.

And then there's the thing I'm most grateful for: one Saturday night in August, 1977, I met Cata.

CHAPTER 15

Cata

It's funny how we met. At least, I think it's funny.

I was working on the deck. We'd do a month in the casino, a month in the discotheque, a month in the lounges, and the month on the open deck. On the deck I was always with Teddy Cochran, who was there permanently. He was my roommate, a senior steward. He'd been on the *Arcadia*. A little tubby guy, married with two children. A friend.

And one night, Cata came on deck. There was nothing for me to do, otherwise. At night, we could pack all the lie-lows and chairs away, and Saturday morning they don't show up until lunchtime. So they don't need the open deck. All the meals would be inside on Saturday, so I'd effectively have the whole day off.

But I still got paid for it. *Bloody marvelous.*

(We'd get paid every three months, and anything over eight hours a day I'd get paid overtime for.)

So Cata's on the top deck of the ship, her mother had gone down into the cabin. And I'd been ashore, out drinking. I was in my whites, which I'd wear even onshore, with a nice silk shirt.

We're in San Juan Harbor; from the ship, you could see El Morro, the old Spanish fortress. And I'm talking to this very attractive woman on deck. I've always had a weakness for auburn haired women. So I said, —By the way, madam, if you don't know the history of the local people here...

(Remember, I have no idea who this woman is. It's not as if she looks Spanish, for heaven's sake.)

—...what happened was, years ago, the natives were fighting the soldiers at the castle, and they'd climb up the outer wall, and when they'd reach the top, those bastards over there (I wouldn't use that word of course) would just hit them on the hands and knock them down like Humpty Dumpty. All of them, killed! That's how the soldiers won the war.

This is *exactly* what she said to me, which I'll never forget as long as I live, God bless her: —I've never heard such a load of *twaddle* in my life. I just need to tell you, I am part of the Tourist Bureau for Puerto Rico. And tomorrow, I will be with the captain, and we can discuss your attitude and your condition, and that you are obviously intoxicated. And you will be dealt with then.

And she just walked away! This is Saturday night.

The next day, I wake up around seven to set up the chairs and such. Toward lunchtime, I see this woman again, and her mother with her. And she called me over. —By the way, I want to discuss with you what you said to me last night. But I'll leave it later. I've decided (because you were intoxicated) not to put it in front of the captain *yet*, but rather to wait and see what happens at the end of the trip.

Every day of the cruise I'd see her. And we'd talk a bit, and she'd threaten to have me fired.

We got on quite well.

That Friday night, I saw her on the deck of course. —You will be seeing me again, she said, —because you will be waiting outside the ship a week from Saturday at ten in the morning, to be picked up and given a *proper* tour of the island.

A week from Saturday she showed up in a big blue American car, a convertible. —It's my birthday on Friday, she said.

—Well, if you come to St Thomas on your birthday, I'll buy you lunch.

And that's how we met.

I wasn't the one who wanted to get married. Cata did.

It turns out she'd gone onboard ship because she'd been injured in an accident in Brazil, and was recovering. People with money recover by going on cruises, I suppose. She told me her birthday was coming up, so I bought her a tea set; I think I gave her the impression I had money. I think she was on the rebound a bit, and I had the world at my feet in those days: I had no debts, would get flown places by Cunard for my breaks. It hadn't dawned on me then that I *could* settle down. I always figured I *would* do so, but I never got around to it until Cata came along.

I used to get a month's vacation on the ship, and I'd go visit a different woman each week, who'd invited me to their homes or holiday homes. I had black curly hair, and nearly everyone else on the ship was gay, so that worked out well for me.

Well, I'd just come back from staying with a young woman – well, not young, it was her teenage children who were young. She'd been married to a Welshman; I suppose she liked that I was English. She wanted to marry me. She could have been a professional tennis player. To give you an idea: she lived four doors down from Paul Newman, in Westport, Connecticut, with two white bearskin rugs in the bedroom – with the heads still attached, facing each other. Her parents owned something nearby. The local newspaper, maybe?

The point being, I'd never have to work again...but I wanted to have children someday, and while I *liked* her children, she was satisfied with just the two.

At any rate, I broke it off and came home to Puerto Rico, where the ship was based. Cata lived two miles away from the port. She used to come pick me up in the car and take me back to the condominium. Well, her cousin and friend Beba was there. They lived together from time to time.

And in front of Cata, Beba said to me, —Where've you been?

—Well, I've known this woman for some time, we've corresponded.

I told the story, and said it was over. Beba asked, rather pointedly, —Why did you not consider getting married?

—I'd like to have children of my own.

—And how old are you now?

—I'm forty-three.

—So aren't you leaving it a bit late?

A bit late?

Honestly, I hadn't given it a thought. I was quite happy, I was making money, I had the best job in the world, a great suntan. I didn't think I was missing anything. But then—

So we arranged that Cata would fly to St Thomas on Fridays to see me. It was only a 20-minute flight. She'd fly with a chap named Mad Jack. He wouldn't land at an airport, he'd land on the beach. Not to be confused with Maureen O'Hara's husband, who – oh never mind, you don't know that reference.

So Cata would fly from San Juan to St Thomas with Mad Jack. We were 'courting,' as they say. Do they still say that?

Beba lived 300 yards from us on the Condado in San Juan. You could look out the front window of our condo and see the *Countess* going by, leaving port; if I were onboard, I'd wave goodbye. I went to see Beba at her condominium once: the apartment had a brass bed and a coffee table and silver set, and if I'm not mistaken, nothing else. I'll always remember her saying to me, —Wally, I've got *five dollars* in my pocket.

I laughed; I had one of my lightweight South African suits on. —Well, I've got a few bucks, I said.

She laughed, then. I didn't realize that the little bits of jewelry on her hands were probably worth more than I made in a year.

Cata's mother's sisters, the Aunties, loved me. So did Beba. They treated me so well. (Don't forget, I had black curly hair, and didn't give two shits about things, which you might say has a certain appeal.)

The history of my wife's family is so interesting to me, though I'm not well informed. I don't talk about my own family's history so much, because I don't *know* it. Cata came from a large family, but also a deep one. They go back many generations, and stayed close.

In my wife's family you have two extremes, Mama's family and Papa's. Papa and his family came from nothing, and didn't want any money off Mama's family. He wanted to be able to pay for everything himself. That's how *he* was. I think we understood each other in that way.

Cata's family lived in completely different world to mine. I'd always wanted to get married, but if I'd not been pushed into it, I might not have done. I was just happy-go-lucky, which sounds more decent than 'lunatic.' I was oblivious. And why not?

I mean to say, my world was my world. I didn't realize I had the chance to enter a different one altogether.

Kathleen was my light.

I want everyone to know about her. That's one reason I've told these stories: I get to talk about Cata, how *good* she was. How strong.

When we moved to Ellicottville, 12 years after we got married, I'd had a janitorial business for several years in Texas. I worked as a soccer official, and as a nurse's aide. For a while I had three jobs. We had a hard time – but I'd seen hard times as a boy, remember. Cata's family had money, *old* money.

But she worked like a dog every day, without resting. When things were tightest, I remember Cata driving to Texas – across the country – to sell a silver set. We didn't have any money to spare then. She was so astute; all that she did was to create a foundation for us to survive. She improved everything that we had, always. We had our differences in things, but I never doubted her.

After she had kids, she stopped wearing nice dresses and such. She was so beautiful inside, attractive outside, so intelligent – but the way she dressed didn't go with that. I've never understood that choice, because for me it *wasn't* a choice: you dressed as well as you could.

The same applies to my son Wally, actually. He won't mind me telling you he dresses like a chimney sweep half the time. (My youngest, Phillippe, knows what he's doing with a suit and tie.)

No matter.

Cata was the Rock of Gibraltar. (*This* time I just mean the turn of phrase, not the actual rock.) I could never have survived without her. She certainly didn't gain anything by marrying me, except children. Well, and I had black curly hair. I was completely opposite to what she was, the life that had surrounded her. It's odd in a way, to think that she chose *me*.

When I'd get angry with her, I'd shake my fist and yell, *You, you, you!!* And she'd stand in front of me and say calmly, regally, like a queen, —My name is *Kathleen*.

That was all it took.

The people in Ellicottville recognized my sons' intelligence, which I wasn't always in a position to see – but I think they also recognized my wife's. That meant even more to me, in a way. I wanted to be accepted in the village, and at times in my life it's been hard to *feel* accepted, but I get by; it was more important to me that people see Kathleen the way I did. She worked three jobs in Ellicottville the same as I did –she was *needed*. She was...all I could see.

Her family were extraordinary as well. Meeting them was like being in yet another new world; I had to pick things up as I went along, to avoid embarrassing my wife.

I wanted her family to accept me as well. It meant so much for people like them to welcome someone like me into their home and their world. I have my pride, but at times I didn't feel like I belonged.

But with my wife, I never had to feel that way.

I gained so much confidence being with Kathleen. When I worked on the *Countess,* we'd go out with Teddy Prince and Teddy Cochran, and they recognized something in her. Teddy Prince was a very smart man, and saw what was special about her right away. And Teddy Cochran *adored* her. But the guys on the ship felt...inferior, in a way. She'd come onboard to see me on a Saturday night, have a drink with me until the boat sailed, and they'd tease me afterward: —Bloody hell, Wally, *she's* a smart one...

But the money never mattered to Cata. In a way that's the most extraordinary thing. She came from luxury but she didn't need it: her drive was all for our *children.* They were the only incentive she needed in life. And in every way her dreams were fulfilled.

And I got the benefit of that, because they were my children as well.

We were all lucky to have her.

'Lucky' and 'easy' aren't the same thing, are they.

There were Papa and Mama, Cata's parents. They didn't object to me marrying her. But they had strong feelings about it. Philip began to accept me after a few years of the marriage, but Ena was Spanish – old-fashioned, and not the way the Irish are old-fashioned, either. She didn't trust me at first, and it took her some time to accept me.

I've carried that feeling for many years.

When Papa died shortly after we moved to Ellicottville, I assumed the boys would get something for their education. But things had gone on, and that money never came to us.

I know Cata was disappointed – her whole life she thought she'd live in one world, and ended up in another – but she never talked about it afterward, *not once.*

We made do, and better: we made a good life.

But all that happened much later, didn't it. After all this time I was so glad to be able to talk about Cata that I've gone and skipped over 15 years. Where was I? I remember...

We married each other *twice.*

In November 1977, Cata and I were married by a judge – I left Cunard on a Saturday and was married on Sunday.

There was a bad omen: as I was backing off the ship, I ran into the ship rail with my back, and my legs went out from under me: total paralysis from the waist down. Papa got me cortisone injections, if I remember right, and the next day I was fit to be married.

Many years later I had cortisone shots again – I got the shots in the morning and officiated a soccer game in the afternoon. Amazing what they can do with a needle. But now my doctor says I'm finished with them, due to my age. I've been exceptionally careful around gangways since then, which hasn't been too hard, as I live 500 miles from the sea.

(I could use those shots today, but with a pacemaker my doctor won't let me have them. As the French say, *C'est la vie.*)

We paid for my family to come over – Amy, Anne, and my niece and nephew, as well as Bob and his wife. Flights both ways and a week's vacation in Puerto Rico. It was quite a break for them.

After the wedding with the judge, by Mama's instructions, I wasn't allowed to share a bedroom with my new wife. Across the road was a guest house, owned by a young couple. Nice people – we ended up being quite friendly with them. I had to stay there for the two weeks. I wasn't allowed to go home.

A romantic start to our married life together.

Then the insurance company wouldn't insure me. Looking back, I think it was my lifestyle: working on the ship, traveling around, and with AIDS just appearing... But I'd had my medical exam, was perfectly fit and so forth. Papa sent me to two specialists. Neither of them could find anything wrong with me. And – not to be coarse – believe me, they *looked.*

I was going to get a third examination, this from an Indonesian doctor. He knew the two doctors who had examined me, so he only looked at me briefly. He said, —Mr Holland, some mornings I wake up and I don't know what's wrong with *me,* and I'm a doctor. There's nothing wrong with you. Go out that door and enjoy living.

I did.

Still, at this point I'm sleeping in a guest house for two weeks before I can have a normal wedded life, I've been warned not to touch the jewelry, and on top of everything they're saying 'Make sure he doesn't have AIDS.' I don't think Mama *disapproved* of me, exactly, but she certainly gave me the third degree.

So I said to both Mama and Papa: —By the way, there's something I want you to know. I only went to school for four years. I wish I'd had more. But I've seen the world, a bit. And there's no shortage of women who would like to marry *me*. I'm a decent human being, which I hope I can prove to you in the near future.

They were always skeptical.

Cata said to me years later, —They know now that they were wrong. About you.

I said they'd never mentioned it to *me*.

—No, they never will.

All the same, I'm glad that they knew.

The great day arrived: 2 December 1977.

Bob and I went to the wrong church.

When we got there, a woman came out and said, —*¿La boda de Holland?* (Spanish for: *Oh, it's you two idiots*) and gave us directions. I think she was a nighttime servant.

Eventually we made it to the right place.

As I understand it, this was one of two local churches which had been donated to the Catholic church by one of Kathleen's aunts. That makes sense: what sort of aunt doesn't have a church or two lying around, after all?

Cata's dress was made by a local designer who lived on the floor below us, in the apartment building. A lovely dress. The designer was connected to Nono Maldonado, a very famous designer in Puerto Rico and friend of ours whose circle we'd become part of. We'd go to fine parties and Cata was able to dress accordingly: cocktail dresses, jewelry. She looked wonderful. In later years she didn't have a chance to dress up that way – you don't put on a fancy dress to cook dinner or teach school. But for parties, in those days, she was like Cinderella. The prize of the ball.

The ex-governor of Puerto Rico, Luis Ferré, was to be the spokesman at my wedding – I had no idea. I knew the kind of family Cata came from, but I suppose I didn't fully realize quite how *grand* things could be.

As Bob and I walked into the (correct) church, I saw an older gentleman holding two silver goblets filled with champagne: one marked 'Catalina,' one marked 'Wally.' We'd had them made, for the wedding. Bob and I had just come from the *wrong* church, we'd been running all over town wondering if I'd be late to my own wedding, and putting it mildly, I needed a drink. So I said to him, —Oh, I'll have one of those, thanks.

I didn't know who the man was, honestly. Kathleen walked over. —He's not offering you a drink, she said. —That's the governor of Puerto Rico.

After that superb introduction we were friends. Luis Ferré always called me 'Walter,' quite nicely I thought.

Later on, I became friends with a Cuban friend of the family. We'd have drinks together. And he'd sell me paintings and prints, fairly cheap. My favourite was a framed print of a woman in a red hooded robe, which I put up in the new apartment. It looked fabulous. (I'm looking at the print right now, in fact.)

Luis came to see my sons, Wally and Phillippe. We called him 'Uncle Louie.' He looked at the print and said, —Oh, I like that.

I told him (quite pleased with myself) it wasn't expensive. —Oh, I know, he said. —If you come to my office on Wednesday, I'll show you the original.

No one wants to be made to feel foolish, but sometimes a little embarrassment does you good.

The original is hanging in the art museum in Ponce now, which Luis founded. I don't mind saying that the original is *even* nicer than the print.

Our wedding rings were made from old gold bracelets that Cata had. They were expensive, at the time – not to Cata, who was used to it, but to me. The reception was held at the yacht club, with orchids picked just that morning.

If they were trying to impress me, they succeeded.

Our honeymoon was three weeks in the British Virgin Islands; in retrospect that seems like quite a long time. I didn't know Cata that well, even then. I think I'd known her about six months. I was in *awe* of her. The languages she spoke – Spanish, French, Italian – the way she moved through the world. I had so much respect for her. I've always been impressed by people with good educations. And she was a great swimmer, while (I think I've mentioned this) I'm not. —*Keep your eye on me!* I'd tell her. Not bragging, mind you – I wanted her to make sure I didn't drown.

In Virgin Gorda, there was a place called Little Jack's, I believe, owned by some Canadians. Some horses to ride – you'll recall my equestrian background, I'm sure. Virgin Gorda has these gigantic rocks, very round, as if they've come from another planet, on a beach called The Baths. Not a bad way to go, if you're a poor swimmer! Fortunately, I survived.

Maybe that should have been the title of this book: *Fortunately, I Survived.* Or 'Unfortunately,' if that's the way you feel about it.

One more story about Cata: In 1994, Cata told me, —I've sold the timber on the hill to pay for a trip to Europe.

I thought, *Great!* I hadn't traveled in Europe in some time.

She said, —Well you won't be going. You'll be looking after the dog.

I suppose I blinked.

She gave me $300. —If you feel like going out for a coffee, or a drink.

She'd planned everything, every detail. I had to laugh. I laughed so much with her, over the years. I don't think my sons even understood that, because by the time they were old enough to start seeing her as herself, she was working so hard all the time.

In England when I was child, we'd walk around at night with a torch, a flashlight, to see by. Cata was like that, as a human being. She was my light.

CHAPTER 16

Dreams

'You'll be looking after the dog.'

That was typical of Cata: her humour, and her focus on the boys. We were married, committed, we loved each other – but the boys came first. Everything for them.

When you have someone with her determination, her intelligence, the *gifts* she had... Cata changed me. She not only looked after the boys, she also looked after me. You might say I was taken into custody when I got married. She dominated the household, and I didn't mind at all. For one thing, I wasn't in England. I had nobody nearby, no family. In England, I would have been ashamed: 'She's got you pinned down,' they'd say. But with Kathleen, I loved every minute of it, because it was an *education* in itself – nobody could have had a better education than me, to be with our two sons and Cata. To be surrounded by *learning.*

I never had any education. To me, it's the ticket out of...well, whatever you're in.

(Actually, I do have one educational achievement to my name: I got a certificate in Spanish from the University of Puerto Rico. It's the only diploma I've ever received, and I'm not ashamed to say that the only Spanish I remember now, for the life of me, is *¿Donde está el baño?*)

Money's not important to me now. I respect it and don't waste it, and I'll have a little of Cata's pension to leave the boys. For such an intelligent woman to have to do three jobs – teacher, musician, working in the church... I can't waste that money. She'd had so much, grown up amongst wealth in the upper class; and then to do all that she did, work so hard only for her children, is still unbelievable to me.

I idolized her. I respected her. I've known people who've lived hard lives and worked hard; *I've* worked hard, God knows. But everything Cata wanted to do, she achieved, because she was never selfish. She gave the boys an education and left me enough to go on with. And she enjoyed it!

If we'd been younger, or other people entirely, we might have said, —Oh let's spend every cent.

But where am I going to go on vacation that I've haven't been? What am I going to see?

I had five dreams in my life, and – how many men can say this? – *every one of them came true.*

I wanted to play soccer for a professional club, and I played as an amateur for City. I was too involved with sex and alcohol to be good enough for the professional team, but what can you do. And I'd have been no good on television anyhow; my ears stuck out and I had a blob nose, and – well, English teeth. I remember one particular girl said to me: —There's something about you that's a bit different, Wally. You're *rugged.*

I suppose she meant I looked like the side of a mountain.

I was a movie buff, crazy about them. I dreamt of being in a picture but I didn't think it was possible. I'd watch *Goodbye Mr Chips* – I never knew until a few years ago that Robert Donat was from Withington, the same district I lived in. And there he was in the movie I loved. (Big world, small world. I can't tell anymore.)

I dreamt of being in a movie like him, and I was, in *The Red Beret* with Alan Ladd. Not quite a starring role, because they didn't want me stealing Mr Ladd's spotlight. (I'm one of the blurry tommies being told we're going to Africa, about an hour into the film.)

I wanted to travel, and I've been to most parts of the world, from South America to the south seas, Africa, Israel, Japan, all across Europe, and now the States. So many people would kill to have a *day* like that, and I spent so many years traveling...

I wanted to be a performer, a choreographer. I have *not* been a choreographer, to date...but I danced with the Supremes in 1976 at a Holiday Inn in Puerto Rico. Now, I was at a party with seven other people, and I acknowledge that I was on the way to being intoxicated. But I made a good show of it. And in recent years I've done nearly ten plays here in Western New York.

I volunteered for Korea. I wasn't brave, just wanted better food.

I loved Greer Garson with great devotion (from afar), and Lana Turner from even farther – though with Ms Turner I was older, and she was more of a sensuous object, if I'm being honest.

My eldest son Wally went to the National Spelling Bee twice, and to MIT. (That's where I had a sit-down with the South Korean Defense Minister – by which I mean I sat next to him. We didn't hold negotiations or anything.) To see Wally there, representing our village and our family, I was the proudest man in the world. When my youngest son Phillippe was valedictorian, and when he graduated from Georgetown and again from law school, I felt the same pride. The world we come from is small – starting with nothing – but you can make something greater for yourself. I believe it.

For a time I believed I might be the oldest soccer official in the United States. I'm the oldest in New York State, I know; I'm 84 this year, still blowing the whistle when needed. There can't be many older in the whole country, though Wally showed me an article on the Internet about a 90-year-old official – good for him.

I believe Cata would be proud of me. I wish I could tell her I'd made it to the very top, that I'd been the oldest in the States, but I think she'd be proud all the same.

...

Did I mention the fact that when I was demobbed and visiting the house of ill repute, I—

I suppose I did. Alright, I'll tell you this one instead.

Did I mention the Scotsman who picked a fight with me in the Ordnance Corps? I smacked him, he hit me, and I smacked my head on the concrete and went unconscious. And when I came to, he drew a knife—

I realized that he was more frightened than I was. He was expecting to get a walk-over, because I was at least a stone lighter in weight, but I gave him a crack instead.

That's not one of the five dreams, mind you. I just 'threw it in there,' for spice.

Friends

I had a bit of a business in the Caribbean, and – well, you don't need details about that, do you. Suffice it to say, I traded in the *green leaf*...

Aloe vera, of course. What did you think I was talking about?

Sid Yuens, my dear friend, made some connections for me. In fact he sold most of my skin-care stuff to the fellows he knew on the ship. They were my best customers. Sid knew everyone – he arranged for Cata and me to have lunch with Oliver Messel, a great friend of Noël Coward's and uncle to Antony Armstrong-Jones, who married Princess Margaret.

Sidney told me he'd sold some skin-care products to Oliver, who loved them, and was apparently interested in buying the business. (It didn't pan out; two weeks later Messel passed away.) He lived four doors away from Claudette Colbert. You *young* people have never heard of her, I imagine. Cata and I went and had lunch with him, outside his house.

Oliver Messel was one of the best-known men on Barbados. It's a pity we didn't manage to do business. But as I say, he had places to be.

Sid Yuens, now. The best dressed man I've ever met in my life – immaculate. Good-looking man as well. When he was on vacation from the ship, rather than go back to England, he'd stay with Cata for a month. I'd go home and he'd be in the spare room. He used to look after our sons as well.

He had a dark side to him. He was very popular – he'd buy things in Colombo and sell them in Puerto Rico. Sidney sold quite a lot of jewelry for Beba – and she never got quite as much money as it was worth. He was on a 'commission,' you see. He was a little bit...cunning. But I loved the guy. After Oliver died, Sidney became the liaison to his nephew Armstrong-Jones.

He had a flat in London. Most of the guys I worked with, they were quite financially sound, with a nice standard of living. They made a good living on ship as room stewards: to put it crudely, they worked their bollocks off, but they made $700 to $1,000 a week. In *gratuitities,* I mean – it's nothing to get $50 a room at the end of the week's cruise, and have sixteen rooms. (This was 1980, mind you.)

Sometimes they'd allow the locals, black guys from Grenada, to help out in the rooms of a Saturday. All the cabins turned over then, so it was the busiest day of the week. And the locals could make more in that day's work than they could in a month on the island. And if there were other favours that could be performed for the guests, well – say no more.

Sidney was like a cog, in a way. Cata bought my gold cufflinks off Sidney, beautiful stuff, for $35 I think. When Sidney went on vacation, you were guaranteed that he'd bought most of his stuff in St Thomas – Dom Perignon for $5, that sort of thing. Whatever he took home would go to profit, or to maintaining his standard of living. He loved caviar – when he threw a party, you could always take some home if you wanted.

They don't get any higher than Sidney. He came from Rochdale in Lancashire, which is known for two things: Gracie Fields, the greatest singer in England besides Vera Lynn (in wartime), and something else. I think Sidney's family *knew*

Gracie Fields, come to think of it. An educated family. Even the way he spoke was refined. I loved him. He loved our whole family. And our condominium on the Condado was to his liking, of course.

A lot of the lads would come in for Saturday night on the ship, whether or not I was there – Cata loved to have eight people at the table, with the nice silverware and that, and they'd all bring bottles of wine...

That was the *reason* for all the extra work, you see. So we could have nights like that, surrounded by friends.

At my age you don't often look back and fondly recall your side business in skin-care products, but it did well. I even went to London to try and expand on the product, and stayed with Pat and Alex – which I *do* fondly recall.

My dear friend Pat owned the Prince of Wales pub in London. (Inside the pub, they had a dress of Florence Nightingale's for some reason. The dress doesn't figure into this story in any way; I'm just making what we call a 'historical connection.')

He and Alex were gay gentlemen who lived together for years. Mum would invite them to the house, even when I was away at sea. On a Saturday night we'd invite them over with their friends, maybe six people. A good crowd. Some money. Now, Pat had a coat made for Alex. A fur coat, double-breasted, with big, unusual lapels. Beautiful – well, not just anything was good enough for his Alex. He had a gold coin as well that he'd carry around, an inch and a half across. 'For my Alex.' I remember Pat did a painting of Winston Churchill once. Terrible, but at least you could tell it was him.

Now, we go to Harrod's together. Alex was prancing a bit, performing. —Ooh, it's *cold*... And we go into Harrod's and it's *five pounds* for morning tea. That was still a lot of money! I got a pound a week in the Army. It was a lot of money to *me*, anyhow. Well, we arrive, and Alex has brought some attention to us. It was a bit embarrassing. And when we walked in to Harrod's, I'll always remember: they'd put a fur coat on special sale. But they'd made a mistake and left a zero off the price. So it was there for £100. There was a big controversy, but they had to sell it at that price. And of course Alex had been wearing fur when he walked *into* Harrod's in the first place.

They took me to a part of Soho, up these very narrow stairs – a heavy man would have had to go up sideways. The door unlocks, we're allowed into the room. And inside there's a very big double bed. Scarlet and leather. The walls were scarlet as well – and hanging on the walls was a hammer, a whip – several whips, I think. The room belonged to a friend of Pat and Alex, a *businesswoman*. She used to get £200 a day.

I suppose she earned it.

Oliver Messel gave Sidney connections to sell my product. Everybody spoke well about it. I had the samples, $1,000 of samples. 'You don't have to buy it, just try it,' I'd say. That went down well. I'd do half the customer's face, which would tighten up nicely, so they could feel it. But the goods didn't look that nice on the table.

Sidney was also introduced to Nono Maldonado, a head man at *Esquire* who was on the judges' panel at the Miss Universe competition. In 1970, Miss Universe was from Puerto Rico; her husband was the agent who sold us our house. They wanted to go on the cruise ship on a Saturday night, so I took them with me, and Cata too of course. I introduced them to the lads, and made sure they understood she was part of *our* party. They went mad, of course.

Nono Maldonado and Cata had known each other for years. I had an evening jacket made there, a cream-coloured double-breasted jacket, which I gave to a friend who lived down the road.

That was our 'scene,' as they say. I like to picture Cata setting out her fine china, the door to the balcony open, breezes blowing, and Cata absolutely in her element – in a roomful of gay men straight off the ship. I suppose if I'd been a different sort of man I'd have been in heaven as well! But you know, I *was* – because Cata was, and because we had friends all around us. It was a good life.

Cata would always look so beautiful for these parties. And of course she had nice stuff to wear then: antique jewelry, nice dresses. That was a different side of her, which our sons never got to see. Once they were born, they were our lives.

The chap who lived above us at Playa Grande was a clothing designer – he made Cata's wedding dress. I gave that away years later, after Cata passed away, to a friend who works at the bank. There was no point in keeping it, and someone else needed it. So off it went.

I think of these stories a bit like that. Off they go.

Sidney dressed like a lord. The last I heard, he was the butler to an old lady in Switzerland. He'd make a lot of money out of that, would Sidney. He'd see to it. And not only what she'd leave him, either. He was a wonderful, refined gentleman. I'd love to contact him again, but I've not been able to find him. For all I say it's a small world, I've managed to misplace him in it all the same.

Freddy Cochran had been my cabinmate on the ship to Japan. He was married to a very beautiful woman named Margaret, with a son and a daughter; when he passed away they wrote to me. I never did meet them, but Tony Hobin did. I think I introduced them, but they kept in touch. They were both amicable people, good humoured. Freddy's wife had cancer later on; Tony went to the funeral, as they'd gotten on socially.

When I worked in Cornwall, Tony would go to see my father, and take him a box of Carr's Biscuits – he liked to talk to my dad, and he had a car. He was an intelligent lad, but he never got the money he should've done, never had the job he should've had. He was also the manager of our soccer team, Melford Celtic, which was the most important thing for him: Tony knew Dave McMurdo, who told Tony about me, and Tony asked me to play for the team. Dave and I were the two best players on the team. I don't say that with any ego, just reflecting what we were capable of. Dave played fullback, I was wing half or forward.

Tony was the type of person who, if you couldn't make a meeting to pay your fees, he'd go and pay them for you. A smashing fellow. He even came to Texas to see Cata, and wheeled my sons all over the place when they were babies.

Tony was involved with a nurse many years ago; I never discussed it with him, but he never bothered with women after that. He should have been a priest – he was very religious, even went to Rome to see the Pope. When he came back to England he was telling everybody about it: 'Don't forget to go see him,' that sort of thing.

Tony passed away with something in his tummy. He was quite young actually – well, I would say he was young. In his fifties.

After the ship went on mutiny, Freddy had been with Cunard for years. He didn't agree with the union – I agreed, they were stoking people's fear. Unions can be like that. I represented the union with Cunard at one point, but I didn't do it because I was a dead union man, I did it because the union representatives had gone on vacation. But someone had to speak for them.

In later years, the unions lost their power, had it taken away you might say, which changed things.

The point is, after the mutiny occurred on the Countess, Freddy was out of work. That was a hard thing.

Freddy died years later with cancer. He was a good man, and I miss him.

You could never hope to meet three more genuine people than Freddy Cochran, Tony Hobin, and my dear friend Bob Butrows. Well, *I've* never met any. (Whereas Sid was a good man, I loved him dearly, but I could never *know* him the same way.) If I were to pass away tomorrow, that would be the one thing I'd want to have said: how much I respected those men. If nothing else had ever happened to me in my life, the chance to thank them and give respects to them would be reason enough to have written this book.

Sid, Tony, Fred: Cata *loved* them. She cherished them. They were good pals of mine, of course, but it means something special that she loved them as well.

CHAPTER 17

Family, Texas

My eldest son, Walter Gerard – named after Dad – was born in 1979. He arrived early, but grew stronger over time, and lost the red hair he was born with. He was surrounded by family: Mama and Papa, aunties, cousins. I kept working, Cata took care of Wally, and we were happy. Honestly, I was happier than I'd ever been. The pregnancy was difficult for Cata but she wanted a family more than anything, and she was happiest of all of us.

In those days I had fewer adventures, you might say, but taking care of a baby is an adventure in itself.

Two babies, even moreso. Our youngest son was born 18 months later, and we named him Phillippe Gerard, after Cata's father Philip.

In 1982 we moved to Spring, Texas, an hour north of Houston on I-45 – and left at Christmas 1989 to live in Ellicottville, an hour south of Buffalo on Route 219.

We first moved to Texas because Phillippe, less than two years old, developed a serious heart condition. Papa suggested the DeBakey clinic in Houston, one of the best in the world, and there was no question that we'd go. I had to leave the ship, of course – Cata contacted them about it. I was working in Barbados, and got word that we needed to leave that very night, because of Phillippe's condition. One of the chaps aboard ship,

Fred (Teddy) Prince, drove me to the airport, looked after me, and helped me get all my things off the ship.

Now, Teddy Prince was an educated man. I'd surmise he was in his late 50s then, I think divorced, from a good family. He got me onto the plane in a proper hurry. As a young man twenty-five years earlier, he'd been pals with Peter, who became captain of the *Countess*. Teddy would do the captain's party on a Sunday night; four people would stand against the wall with trays of champagne, another four waiter going around with drinks, offering anything the guests wanted – all of it free, of course.

The captain would come into the lounge, would greet the 'important' passengers. He'd be with the purser, first officer, chief engineer, the cruise director. Then Peter would walk up to Teddy and say, —Oh Teddy, how are *you* tonight?

Teddy had had a couple of drinks, of course, and he's standing there holding these champagne glasses. —Would you like a drink, sir?

The captain replied, —No thank you Teddy. Can I buy *you* a drink?

—With all respects, sir, I never drink with the crew.

Can you imagine, saying that to the ship's captain? Of course, they had been young together, and Teddy Prince was a well-spoken man, educated, gifted. With a little 'tache like David Niven.

He could get away things like that. And it doesn't hurt, being a friend of the captain's.

I tell you about Teddy because it's easier than talking about when Phillippe was sick.

Cata prayed for him every day. She prayed and offered to say a rosary every day, if only he would get well. She had prayed for Wally when he was only little, and prayed again, every day, for

Phillippe. We gave them both the name 'Gerard,' after Saint Gerard.

As a newborn baby Phillippe was small and frail. Both times Cata was pregnant there were complications, but she wanted children more than anything.

Phillippe had a hole in his heart. A hole in his *heart,* can you imagine? Of course we were terrified.

Talking about it is hard, even after all this time.

The day before the operation the doctor came into the hospital room and asked Cata, —Do you believe in miracles?

She said of course she did, and she was telling the truth.

The doctor was crying. We were *all* crying, to be honest.

He said, —Your son's heart has closed up. Go home, and never come back.

We had to have everything transferred from Puerto Rico to Texas, of course. It was quite an undertaking. We had a Steinway baby grand piano, for one thing, which was damaged in transit. I had a new pair of shoes and some aftershave in the same box as an antique silver coffee set – we never found them. (I was able to replace the aftershave.)

You know, when I married Cata they'd accused *me* of being after the silver. By this point in the story I hope you're on my side, so I can ask: does that seem fair to you?

It was one mishap after another, moving to Texas. First we put down a large deposit on a beautiful house near a golf course, very much sought after. It flooded and became a disaster site. We looked at Spring instead, put down a few thousand more on a rental, and finished up losing the money, because we had bought a house that was being built new, and we didn't stay through our entire term...

Our next-door neighbours made swimming pools. (My son tells me this is a 'colourful detail,' which is his way of saying 'Get on with it.') One night, Kathleen came and woke me up, saying, —There's a man downstairs, he's just got into a car outside the driveway...

I saw the guy lying on the floor of the car, in the backseat. That hardly seemed normal. We phoned the police, and they came to the house, saying, —We've looked in the car, there's nobody there.

—There certainly was a minute ago, lying down.

They broke into the house next door and got $18,000.

It seemed strange to me. Cata and I had seen *somebody* get into the car. Were we both wrong? Or did the police know, and not give two shits?

We moved after that.

I didn't have a lot of confidence in the police in Texas, and still wouldn't.

I worked as the night manager at a Denny's in Spring. We used to get the nightclub crowd. There was a particular guy who owned a nightclub, who'd come in with his wife. He used a cane, I remember. They came in quite often for meals, and this particular time, they started arguing, and it got to the point of violence. The police came and took both of them away. When they got into the car, a gun was fired. I don't know the ins and outs of the situation. I do wonder who fired the gun, though.

Another time, I was the assistant manager at a bar called The Stone Crab. It was my night off, a Thursday if I recollect, with three of the staff on. Thieves came in and took $8,000 at gunpoint. Apparently taking things at gunpoint is a decent business in Texas.

There was one fellow who came into the bar, and – well, there are people who see you one time, and want to be overfriendly, calling you by your first name and the like. My main job was to make sure that everybody knew they'd be taken care of; people enjoyed being there. Well, this fellow would come in, and he was a conman. He came in with a gold chain of some kind, nervous: —This is a *bargain*, Wall. I've broken down in a card game, they need my money straight away, I'll give it to you for $40...

Rubbish. I gave him the money, but he'd taken me for a goose and a gander, as you say. I got 'taken around the corner.'

You *always* have something to learn in life. Unfortunately, sometimes you learn it in Texas.

I did get back to England to visit from time to time, in those days. Bob and I were going to Stonyhurst once. I'd never been in the Grand Hotel, so I said to Bob, —Let's go in and have a cup of tea.

The waiter had a thick Lancashire accent, and – well, I've told that story, haven't I.

Anyhow, as I was going to the toilet, Keith Carradine came through. I said, —Aren't you...?

He said yes. I said, —I've just come from Texas.

He said he'd just made a movie about the pope, for television. —What a small world, I said, —that I should bump into you here.

(He probably thought I was mad. I thought *he* was originally from Texas. According to my son, 'Wikipedia' says he's from California. So I was only off by a thousand miles, which isn't bad for an Englishman with four years of schooling.)

And I promised my dear readers I'd tell you about my conversation with Bond, James Bond, didn't I.

I was in the airport in London, leaving for New York (for the sake of argument, let's say it was the same trip) when I bumped into Timothy Dalton, all in black leathers – him, not me. He was about ten feet away. We communicated with head shakes and hand movements, the way old friends do:

Eyebrow raise, head nod, 'quizzical' expression. (*'Aren't you Timothy Dalton?'*)

Chin down, slight shake of the head. (*'No.'*) Finger wag. (*'Don't want to speak.'*)

If I'd been a young man I would have asked him for his autograph. But I was too old for that, and I thought, *I can't be bothered.* I just waved goodbye to him. (*'Goodbye.'*)

The three of us, Dalton, Carradine, and I, all went on to successful acting careers.

Of course Cata and I made friends in Texas. We'd even have them over for parties at the house, and the kids would sleep in their rooms upstairs – not the same as the parties we'd have in San Juan, but then *we* weren't the same either. When you get married and have a family, you become a different person altogether.

Somewhere we met our dear friends John and Sylvia Parker – wonderful people. Sylvia and I still send each other Christmas cards every year. She and her husband used to create these parties, and she'd assign you someone else other than your wife to talk to, mixing and matching people. —Oh talk to *them*, they'll find *you* interesting...

John was a chemist for one of the oil companies – a very good job, obviously. He had a great sense of humour. He wasn't unlike Stanley Holloway to look at, so I suppose he had to. A wonderful human being, quiet and subdued, humble. Everybody loved him.

John Parker died of cancer while we were still in Texas.

It's different, telling stories about your friends after they've gone. It's...deeper, you might say.

There was a blonde girl, divorced and always falling in love with different people. We'd gone to one of her parties. And a guy called Read came up and introduced himself—

Now, my father used to do...well, not an impersonation, since I don't think he knew about it. But the same sort of 'act' as a comedian named Al Read. He was one of our most popular comedians in the early years of the late 50s, or the later mid-50s. Something like that. In his act, he always addressed himself to a person who wasn't there, playing both parts. My father did the same thing when he was telling me jokes, but he did it unconsciously. He'd talk about what had happened when he was working in a mental hospital, laying the floors, and he'd take the part of each person in the conversation, in his voice and mannerisms. Now, Al Read became famous all over Great Britain with his act. He'd pretend to argue with a soccer official, say: —Who, you? You're as blind as a *bat!* And then he'd turn around and play the official. —How *dare* you talk to me...

Now there's this fellow named Read at a party in Texas, of all places. And he's Al Read's son, of course, explaining to me what *his* dad did, as if I didn't know!

My son tells me I repeat myself, but if he has any complaints, he can go work on someone else's memoir instead. And I'll say it again: it's a small world.

I had a janitorial service in Texas, Castle Clean Company. ('Keep Your Castle Clean with the Three C's: Careful, Caring, and Consistent.') A larger company called Castle Cleaners 'suggested' that we change the name, so I did:

'Wally Holland and Sons.'

We were still careful, caring, and consistent, but the business card didn't look as good.

My sons didn't actually have anything to do with the company; I wouldn't have wanted them to. We always meant for their lives to be full of other things.

I had five women working for me. We worked hard and made a decent living. I had a contract to clean the little private school my sons went to for kindergarten and a realty office, and the real estate agents would use me to clean the houses they were showing as well. There was plenty of work to go around, new buildings and houses to clean. I'd work of a weekend – missing soccer games didn't enter into it, there was no soccer on television in America in those days.

I'd rather keep my Saturdays open now, to watch United.

We could do a house over a weekend and make $600 or so. I've talked about being 'nippy,' alert, on my toes. This was one way I could do that; I made something out of that cleaning service, I really did. I'd go to Happy Hour at the bar nearby and have a Bacardi and Coke – two at most – and make business connections there. You can't just take chances, you have to *make* them, even if it means drinking Bacardi in Texas. One day at the bar I met a multimillionaire – I've forgotten his name of course – and I ended up doing his apartment. He had a white carpet, and asked if I could get it clean.

—No, I can't. I can improve it, but I'll do what I can and you can pay me whatever you wish.

Well, I cleaned the carpet, put a lot of work into it. But the one bad spot he had, there nothing I could do with chemicals or a brush. So I *trimmed* the carpet with scissors and improved it. The rest of the house was spotless.

—That's a big difference! he said.

—You can put a piece of furniture over it, I suggested.

—That makes sense.

—It's *common* sense! Anyone who tells you they're going to get a white carpet clean, they're selling you down the river.

He had enough money for nice white carpets, but not enough that he didn't care about being taken advantage of.

—How much do I owe you?

I told him. —You're undercharging, he said.

He gave me three times what I asked for, and said: —Would you like to do my apartments? I own condominiums.

—No.

He was a bit surprised at me saying no to so much work, and money. —Why not?

—I don't have the staff for that – I'd have to hire someone else and put them in charge of it, and I wouldn't want to let you down.

—It's only cleaning.

—No, I said, —That's just the side you see. What's more important than whether we get it clean?

—Whether I can trust you.

—Exactly. I'd worry too much about the people I was sending over. (And I didn't want the hassle, honestly.) —But I'd be happy to come over and tell you some disgusting jokes.

We were friends for quite a while. He was a smashing guy. (I'm not just saying that because he paid me three times the fee.)

You can gain more by being open with people than by being tight.

I remember going into this bar in Houston – I hadn't been in before, actually – and finding a wallet next to the car beside mine. I didn't look inside at first; I went into the bar. Then I opened it up to find out whose it was, and asked the bartender, was Mr So-and-so there?

The bartender called out – the guy was there at the bar. I gave him his wallet, told him I'd found it outside.

The guy was *all over* me. He was ever so grateful.

That's my nature. It's amazing how easily you can get close to someone – how they'll accept you if you help. Whereas powerful people talk about 'diplomacy,' an everyday working man might talk about being 'two-faced.' It's to do with common sense: instead of telling lies, you *deceive* people in a way, put them at ease. The intonation in your voice, the way you lean, you can maneuver people to get what you want, or more often what you *need*. Something as simple as taking your phone out and pretending to speak to someone if you want to avoid someone else – Oh, I'll be there in a moment...and then you get out of there.

It's a case of doing what's needed, really. In my life, that's how it's always been. Jehovah's Witnesses at the door – they're wonderful people, they really are. And you don't want to tell them to piss off, not in so many words. But you do *want* them to piss off. So instead you say: —With all respects to you, I think you do a wonderful job, I can understand it all, and do not wish to discuss my religious life. Forgive me; I wish you a good day. Please leave before I do.

You can be diplomatic. It's not quite honest, but it's not lying, either. It's being...someone *else* for a moment.

When I bought Cata that tea set in St Thomas, she might have thought: *By Christ, he's got a bit of money.* Maybe I meant her to think that. I didn't make a blunder, anyhow; she turned out to be a wonderful woman.

People talk about higher-ups, a sophisticated way of life. When I married Cata, I realized that I was entering a higher level of people than what I'd been used to as a working man. Being so short of education, but *knowing* how much education mattered, instead of resenting it I thought: *I'm so fortunate.* And what I had going for me was that I could blend in. I had a sense of humour about it, and I was willing to learn – I *wanted* to learn, because I didn't want to be an embarrassment to her, or to my family. But in many ways I still am. It's in my fortune, in the stars: I'm a bit 'zany,' and have always felt a little oddly, a little bit outside of the world.

I don't mind.

At the end of each chapter, I feel I should put a bit of wisdom, or a joke, or even something a bit sad. Or I might say, *I have to leave you now.*

We'll try this instead: *I love you. Piss off.*

CHAPTER 18

Home

At Christmas of 1989 we moved to Ellicottville, an hour south of Buffalo in the southwest corner of New York state. When you say 'New York' to an Englishman (or a Texan) he thinks of Times Square and the Statue of Liberty, but Ellicottville is a little ski village in the country, a whole day's drive from New York City.

My sons ask sometimes if I'd ever go back to England. I'll visit one more time, I think, but that's all. The neighbourhoods I grew up in, the buildings are gone, the people have passed on or moved away. I can watch United on my TV, and talk to my friends on the phone. And I can *remember:* telling you these stories, some I've not thought of in fifty years, it's like I've lived them all over again.

Besides, I've no need to go back to England. Here in Ellicottville, I'm home.

When we moved to Ellicottville from Texas, Cata was the leader. She even drove in front during our move: I got sidetracked on the highway in my Isuzu Trooper. Typical. Wally and I tried to cross a divider covered with snow and got stuck for a long time, while Cata and Phillippe waited a few miles down the road. (Cata was a marvelous driver. Good thing, as well – she always insisted on driving, though I suppose that was more to do with her accident, years before.)

It was the first snowstorm the kids had ever seen, though it was *nothing* to what was waiting in Ellicottville. Phillippe and Wally saw their first 'white Christmas' during our move, at a Motel 6 in Kentucky.

I have no memory of this, but Wally wants me to mention that the kids got their first 'Nintendo' at that motel, which I gather is a game of some kind, and he couldn't play it until we'd moved into our apartment in the village, which was *very trying* for him. Merry Christmas, lads.

Wally played me a song once, with a man shouting, 'How did I get here?' (He and I like very different music, I must say.) Well, here's how I got here – to Ellicottville:

Cata was very involved in the church throughout her life. She wanted to become a nun when she was younger; this would be a very different book if she had. The priest who married us was a handsome swine, could have been a movie star. Cata had known him since he was a young man. A friend of ours had come over with her niece, who was a nun taking her final vows to the Church. But the Catholic church wouldn't allow this woman and her niece to stay there. So the priest, who knew Cata, phoned us and asked us to put the two of them up for the evening.

I finished up taking the nun – a good-looking woman in her 20s, by the way – for a walk on the beach late at night. I was just married, and I was fascinated: how did this woman decide to join the church? I can't remember the answer, now.

Cata's cousin Ernesto worked as a coroner in Buffalo, for Erie County, and our friend, the nun's aunt, knew him – through medical circles, I suppose. And the father of our family doctor in Buffalo was a friend of theirs as well — they graduated together from some school or another. Funny old world.

When we had children, Cata wanted to move north. She felt it would be a better life, leaving Texas. In 1989, the time had come to move, and we decided to come to Ellicottville.

We left Texas just before Christmas. Separated on the highway, stuck in snow...the usual foolishness. We moved into that friend's house, in the apartment upstairs.

It went badly. I won't dwell on that.

We found a house on a country road: acres of woods and a beautiful rolling field at the bottom of a hill. We moved on.

I don't talk much about Ellicottville because there's so much *else* to talk about. I've been so many places, so much has happened. But coming here was like coming *home*, a place to rest. My life became more 'normal,' so to speak. When I was single, my life was gratifying — marvelous, really. But when children come into your life, you change mentally, and you begin to want different things.

When I was single, I'd get up in the morning, and everything would be about *me*. I'd go to work, laugh, enjoy life, feel pain — whatever. I was a human being.

But I got married, and from the beginning so much happened. I married into completely different circumstances from what I was used to, and as a result, *I* was completely different. I had to be. You change to fit the life you're living, in a way. And I don't mind.

Ellicottville is a special place. There's so much variety in the community, which you might not expect from such a small village. But we get all kinds here. Even me.

And there's such peace and normality about the place. When you come here you settle into the village, and the pace of the village settles into you. Even Cata – when we first met she used to love wearing cocktail dresses, jewelry, fine clothes, and going out to parties. But here you don't need to put on airs or advertise what you have. People *know* each other, each other's parents and kids. You can't pretend.

In our early life we met such a mixture of people. Gay artists, governors, shipmates. We had a *nightlife.* It was 'cosmopolitan,' you might say. Ellicottville is quieter, and the life of the village still mostly revolves around skiing, which I don't do. But then, I'm older.

(You do meet some fascinating people here, sometimes quite unexpectedly: I once won a little prize for a poem I'd written, and got to attend a writers' conference at Holiday Valley. And who was guest of honour but Anne Perry, the mystery writer who once helped kill a woman in New Zealand? She seemed nice, all things considered.)

Cata had to search for a job when we arrived – she couldn't find a job that suited her qualifications. And Ellicottville is the kind of place where it takes a long time to become a 'local.' But over time, between her education and her personality, she found a place – people understood what she could do.

I do love it though. Ellicottville is a wonderful combination of old families living the way they were and new people with a bit of money living the way they *wish* to. There's a sense of freedom out here.

I've been in the village a long time – longer than I've stayed in any other place, in fact.

Long enough to have made friends here and lost them.

Bob McCarthy was the 'voice of Ellicottville.' Me being Irish, Bob brought out the Irish in me – he'd call out across the street to me, 'Aye aye, Wally Holland!' Always both names, especially when I walked into a room. He's irreplaceable.

Bob was a wonderful friend to the village. He was very laid-back, didn't bother about politics or religion – he was like...a foundation stone.

Joe and Adam Delity were a foundation as well, of soccer in our community. We were soccer officials together; Adam has retired, Joe passed on, so I'm the last of the three young men. Here in the village there's a marker, a slab of rock by the town soccer fields to commemorate Joe. It reads: *Delity Fields*. Having lasted this long as an official, being a bit known in the village and the towns nearby, I feel I'm getting the recognition that *they* deserve. It's only through the work that they did that I'm getting acknowledged.

I used to get asked, —Are you one of the Delitys? (Perhaps because I had white hair like they did, and didn't sound American.) That happened a lot. Adam was a good-looking man, so that wasn't so bad. He still is, actually. But if I'm being honest, Joe left a bit to be desired, *visually* speaking. So I'd slot in between the two of them.

Years ago, Joe would drive me to meetings of soccer officials in Fredonia, since I had no idea how to get there. And he'd put polka on the car radio. Have you ever heard polka? I said, —Joe, do you have a change of record for this? At this point, *I* can do the polka.

Every time I got in the car he'd put the tape on. Am I fan of polka music? I cannot tell a lie, so I will say nothing.

When we first arrived, we were living in an apartment, and I was guided by Cata's decisions. But certain promises never materialized, in terms of work. It took us a while to pull our lives together.

We weren't alone, but we had left Cata's parents behind in Texas, and they passed away a couple of years after we moved.

Cata worked as a substitute teacher in different places, and eventually got a good job – which was essential for us to provide for our sons. My own wages left something to be desired, and I was in a similar situation to some of the working-class people in our area. I did three jobs for a while: returning to janitorial work, working part-time as a nurse's aide, and officiating several soccer matches a week. Cata taught at the schools nearby in Springville, taught piano lessons when she could, and ran the music and religious education programs at the church. It was hard – and it wasn't what we'd expected or planned on as we moved from Texas.

But we were happy. We were completely occupied in work and life, with our two wonderful children to look after. And Cata was so *grateful* to be a parent. Nothing mattered to her as much as Phillippe and Wally, and the way we lived before simply fell away, somewhat. You might say there was too much life to be lived in the present.

And of course Cata had worked so hard to become a mother in the first place.

It wasn't until Wally's first trip to the Spelling Bee in Washington D.C., the respect that we were given in town after articles came out in the paper, that I understood what Cata wanted for our sons in terms of education. Of all things, I gave an interview to one of the TV news programs in Buffalo, standing outside our house. If I remember right, I told them I wanted Wally to be normal, to play baseball, to fall down a bit and get up. And I was *elated* to see him on the stage: to see what *else* life could be, through education, through *that* kind of hard work.

Cata looked after every aspect of the house. She had a dominant character. And I didn't mind at all – I'd been a bit macho, getting into fights when I was younger, and I'd thought so much of *myself* until she came along. But meeting her, and then meeting Wally and Phillippe, my personality changed so much, because I began to want something new out of life. They had shown me what that could be.

When our eldest son was born, Kathleen was lying there on the hospital bed, and she said to me, —As long as I make you happy...

I started crying. You've just given birth to a child, I thought, and to say *that* to me...

I just wanted to lift her up and carry her. What an extraordinary thing, to want that above everything else on that day, to *give happiness* and to give of yourself. But that's how she was.

My sons were spoiled. Well: they had family all around happy to lavish attention on them. But then Cata spoiled them all over again.

I don't mind.

My eldest son was very confident as a boy. Wally had his weaknesses and always will – so many intelligent people, if someone is aggressive with them, will be defiant and almost disgusted: —Oh for *Christ's* sake... It's normal to be impatient, but you don't talk that way to someone who might get back at you. Wally didn't know what to do with that. I'm not made for that either. When I was a lad we'd fight with Marquess of Queensbury rules, which I was fine with – if somebody hit me I could retaliate, because I had a good reason. But I couldn't ever hit someone otherwise.

Oddly enough, the last fight I was in, I ran into five people onboard ship who'd done a dirty trick on me. One of them said something, so he was the one I went for. He was the smallest one, fortunately. When I'd knocked him down I didn't want to hit him anymore – I started crying and said, —Oh for Christ's sake, *go away.*

I finally understood, at that time, that I have a temper that boils within me, gets out, and can hurt people. It took me half a lifetime to realize that, can you imagine?

Phillippe never had that resentment, living in Ellicottville; he was more grounded, maybe because he was younger. He knew how to use his intelligence, but also how to talk to people without being arrogant.

I think the two boys are like me, *both* of them – I look at them and see two sides of myself, in a way. And of course, I see Cata.

I've got to be careful writing this next part, as I get upset thinking about it.

When I married Cata, she was *dominating*, which I don't mean in a bad way at all. She was a wonderful influence and guide, because of her intelligence and humour. With my sons, I never fully understood their minds, how intelligent they both were. She had to *explain* that to me, you see.

I went with her to Texas, when they were testing her for cancer. It was funny, in a way: she'd lost the inheritance she was supposed to get, but a friend in Texas wanted to leave her all the money she had. But Cata said *No* – give it to her relatives. Hundreds of thousands of dollars, I mean. It would have changed our lives.

When I first met Cata, she was recovering from a car accident in which she was very badly hurt, and her cousin's wife was killed. Papa had flown to assist the doctors in her recovery. Afterward he told her: —They'll tell you when you're older that something's shown up on chest x-rays, that you have lung cancer. But don't you believe them – it's scar tissue.

When we went to Texas, after she'd been examined in Buffalo and couldn't believe the diagnosis, it was...not a repudiation, but a real shock. What Papa said to her, it was surely true at the time. And it was hard for her to believe that things had changed.

But she was so strong that she came to terms with the diagnosis better than I did. I've never thought about it until recently: my own Mum and Dad had gone, Uncle Teddy, Amy – everybody of *mine* had gone, and Kathleen was all I had. The doctors confirmed the diagnosis, and we said OK, and went away to try to live with it. When I think of the courage that she had...

Cata showed me a way out of the world I had known. Not with her *money*, but with her way of thinking, of being.

When my own mother passed away, I was only ten years of age. I was heartbroken. I ran across the busiest road in Manchester, and God was with me that I wasn't killed myself. I ran a mile to Unkie's. When Dad passed away he was 74 years old. He said to me: —Son, don't shed no tears for me. I am ready to go.

At my age, I understand how he felt – I'm ten years older now than Dad was when he died. He'd made peace with it. He was a gambler like me – on horses, and soccer. And he said to me at the end, —So-and-so hasn't given me a winner for six weeks, City have been terrible, and my two pals from the pub have died. I'm ready to go, son.

I was working away, coming home from time to time. And I knew what he meant: he felt *isolated*. After he lost his floor-design job, later in life, he just earned a meagre day-to-day wage. I used to send him money every week or two, in case he wanted a drink or cigarettes. Which was fine, I could afford it. And before he passed away, he said, —I'm going in the hospital, son, and don't think I'll be coming back. Don't shed no tears for me.

—And by the way, he said, —Thank you for the money you were sending me. You'll find it underneath the bed and the carpet. There's quite a bit more than you sent me. I picked a few winners.

If you've got a favourite horse, you've got to put a decent amount on it, or it's not worth it. But a horse that's 2:1 on, $20 on to win $10, it'd *better* bloody win, or you're going to have to talk to the trainer. When Dad said he'd backed a few winners, he meant easy money, a little bit at a time.

And he left me more money than I've ever had in my life.

I learned to live with my Mum passing away – I was young, it was hard, but I had time. When Dad passed away I was older, I was away – he said I had my life to live.

When I went to Korea, Dad had taken me to the pub and bought me a couple of drinks. I wasn't even 19 then. When I told him I was going to Korea, that night, he walked with me to the bus. (We never had a car, of course.) He put me on the bus, and he said, —*Make sure you bleeding come back here.*

When Dad said that to me, I realized how he felt – how he'd *always* felt. He'd always taken care of me, and always would, if he could.

A couple of years ago, there was a flashlight in my bedroom on the dresser. It wouldn't work. I woke up at three in the morning, and the light was on, going across the ceiling. I thought: *What the bleeding hell's this?* It had me a bit nervous. I slowly got up, got ahold of the light. It never worked for months, no matter how I tried. And there it was.

The next time I saw Father Mierzwa, he said, —You know Wally, Mary is the lady of the light.

I suppose he was joking in a way, and serious in a way.

Kathleen was my light.

She passed away in 2002; she was 60 years old. The boys came home from school that night and we drank to her.[7] I think of her every day.

I was in the house on my own, once, after Cata had died. And butterflies started coming to me from nowhere, landing on my hands and clothes.

A couple of years ago I won the raffle at the church: $500. That afternoon, I'd gotten there late, and sat down at the end of a table. *Is this seat taken?* and so forth. The lady sitting there was with her husband, and she said no. I asked, —Well, would you like to share with me, in case I win?

She said no thank you. —Oh you don't have to share *yours*, but I'll share mine, if I win.

Again, —No thank you.

But of course I won the top prize.

That seemed odd to me, to offer my winnings to someone I didn't know, and *then* to win.

It may seem like I've gone from one thing to another, but I don't think I have. I've written so many times in these pages that throughout my life I've always been lucky. What I mean is that I've been *blessed*, and I am so grateful.

Cata became very much a part of the community here – the people at the church found out that she had a lovely voice. And

---

[7] Phillippe's friend Bernie drove home with him, fast as they could, from Washington to Ellicottville, and he was there when we got the news about Cata. It was a wonderful thing he did, for my son, and to this day we're grateful.

I think Father Mierzwa appreciated Cata's outlook on life, and her conversation.

...

Have I told you about my wife?

I don't mind telling you again.

She won a medal for being the top student in Montreal, sang with a choir at Carnegie Hall, and worked as a simultaneous translator in the Puerto Rican legislature.

It wasn't as though she was mayor of Ellicottville or anything. She didn't have a dignified position. But I don't think she needed one – she seemed elevated, no matter what she did. Overseeing religious education for our local church – the things she did, they touched people all over the district.

She spoke four languages as well. It's no surprise I'd feel inferior, I've hardly got *one.*

We moved because Cata wanted a better life for our sons than she felt they'd get in Houston.

Wally and Phillippe both finished up outstanding scholars. People still mention them to me, saying they remember them – but not because of academics, oddly enough. They'll mention the plays they performed in, music... They ended up with a love for those fine things. And that was Cata.

I miss my wife.

She guided me in a new direction in life, helped me to be grateful for what I have. I go to church twice a week in respect of Cata; she would have wanted that. It doesn't make me a better Catholic, or even a better person, but it's a chance to show gratitude.

And today, like most days, I'll walk down the street in the village and wave hello to people I know – and around here you know everybody. I shake hands with dear friends at church, see kids on the soccer field and at the school that I knew as babies, swim at the pool at Holiday Valley, visit the library to read emails from my sons. In the mornings I go the gym in Springville, and there's a little community there, and we support each other. From time to time I perform in a play: *Twelve Angry Men, Barefoot in the Park, The Crucible, One Flew Over the Cuckoo's Nest.* (I even got to perform in a play with Wally; I played his dad, which wasn't too much of a stretch.)

At Christmas I visited Phillippe and his wife Jessie in Chicago, and got to play with *his* two sons, Alfie and Frankie. And this summer I'll see Wally and his wife Agi, and their son Feliks. Feliks plays for the Maroon team in the boys' soccer league in Cambridge; Phil has shown me videos of Alfie dribbling the ball, and he's only three years old. Frankie's a bit young for all that, but there's time.

I'm looking out my window right now at the village, the grass outside, the woods, the hills, and I could not choose a better place in the world to be right now. Don't get me wrong, I loved Paris, Vienna, Nice, Puerto Rico, Japan... I've seen a lot of the world, and there's no place I'd rather be than here. I've done and seen all the things I've ever dreamed of, and now I'm home.

Letters and articles

The first of these letters was written for Memorial Day 2014, and appeared in the village paper in Ellicottville. I wanted to put some very strong feelings into words, and asked my son Wally for help. We continued working together. The rest are about football, and other things: getting older, staying young, remembering, forgetting. Our first letter was entitled 'A Word of Thanks,' and you could use the same title for every one of them.

—WJH

A word of thanks

I'm told that at some point, as we grow older, life stops giving us things and begins taking them away. Maybe that's true, or maybe things aren't so dark as all that. But we can give one another thanks. Doing so is a blessing.

Many of my friends in the village are veterans, as I am; and over the years many more have passed on, as people do. I miss them. Last year we lost my friend Rudy LaBelle. Rudy was full of spirit and kindness. He and his wife Ruth have been good to me and my family. He was 88. I wish he were here. I would like to thank him.

Rudy graduated from high school in 1943 and before he turned twenty he had been sent to the Pacific by the US Navy to fight, to kill if need be, and to die if need be. Rudy was lucky: he came back home to Ruth. Lucky twice over.

I imagine young men like Rudy felt like they were saving the world. Maybe they did. I feel like they saved me.

I was five years old when the war began. I was evacuated from my home in Manchester and separated from my family, because planes were coming each day with bombs to kill us all. The German army was right across the Channel. I didn't realize they were so close. It was terrible; but I was a young boy, and it was also exciting. There was war, and terrible villains.

And heroes. That's how we saw the Yanks. When they came they had sharp uniforms and an easy way about them. They looked like movie stars. They'd come from across the ocean to fight with us and for us. It meant the world to me in those days. It still does. We thought that Great Britain stood alone, and then found that it wasn't so.

It is hard for me to talk about.

The war ended. I grew up and moved away, as people do. I joined the British Army and worked at sea, came to America, met my wife Cata, started a family. All these things life has given me.

I miss Rudy. I'd like to tell him thank you today; that time has passed. But I can thank all the men and women who serve others as he did, and spare a thought for those who have gone on without us, who have kept us safe. May they make their way safely to the other shore.

Adam

I've lived in the United States since the late 1970s, but have never become a citizen, by which I mean no disrespect to my adopted home. In any case, I realize that on one important matter I have long since given way: at some point I began to say 'soccer' instead of 'football.' Nobody's perfect.

It's a wonderful time to be a soccer fan in the U.S. I fondly remember coaching children's soccer in Texas in 1982, and have found ways to stay involved in the game since then: as a coach, an official, and a proud supporter of our teams here in Ellicottville. In all that time – has it really been thirty years? – I've never experienced the kind of passion and excitement for the game as we have right now, as the U.S. team pushes forward in the World Cup.

The game I love has found a home here too. This is a great joy for me. My own grandson, Feliks, loves to pretend that he's in the World Cup. My son tells me Feliks likes to play at being Lionel Messi rather than Wayne Rooney.

Nobody's perfect.

Soccer players and supporters in Ellicottville owe much to the efforts of Adam Delity and his late brother Joe to keep the game alive here. It falls to me to pass on a bit of sad news: Adam tells me he will not be emerging this year to officiate; it's time, he says, to hang up his whistle. If you see him in town, tip your hat with me. He has given much of himself to our kids and our village. I'm ever so grateful to him. I've enjoyed staying young with him.

As for me, I think the coming season will be my last as an official. Parents and supporters, I must tell you: as wonderful as it is to watch your children play – I remember it well – it's nothing to the feeling of running downfield with them, witnessing their little triumphs and frustrations up close, being a small part of the moments of foolishness and genius and heartbreak and good fortune that make up this game we love.

Adam and I really have had the best seat in the house. Well: now we get to pass it on. (Ideally to folks with fewer miles on them.)

And that is a joy too.

– WJH

Referee

Summer passes, the weather cools, kids return to their classrooms. I'm off to officiate at another soccer game today, North Collins and Springville. The leaves haven't changed for the season yet, but of course they're always changing. Everything is, a little at a time, or a lot. I've been doing a bit of theatre in Olean and Springville. They say acting is a younger person's game. Well – they say that about everything, don't they. But here I am, changing along with the seasons.

I'm thinking of my friend Joe again, and his brother Adam. Joe was the oldest soccer official in western New York: still young after more than 80 years. Like so many good things, he passed that honour down to his brother Adam. Now I'm pleased and proud to find that it's passed to me, and next year it will fall to someone else. Lucky devil.

What a blessing to be able to share the field with young children. To work hard and to share in their own hard work. At my age, the joy of taking the field is deeper than it used to be: less frantic, perhaps less exciting, but sharing our kids' excitement lifts me up. I hope that I can lift them up in turn.

I wonder whether there are other fellows my age acting as referees for their local leagues. It's hard to know whom to ask. It seems like such a small thing – but enough small things make up a life. The oldest soccer official in America. Can you imagine? It's a nice thought on a Monday in September, anyway.

And now it's time to get ready for the game.

Regards,
Wally Holland Sr.

German

Telling your stories, even little ones, starts to feel a little like paying a debt – you're so fortunate to have gotten them in the first place. And it keeps the mind sharp, even if I take the corners a little more slowly than I used to.

Yesterday I refereed a game in Hinsdale. Absolutely wonderful. Maybe it's the excitement of the World Cup lingering a bit, maybe it's nothing more than a new batch of young students joining the teams, but the spirit and technique on both sides were superb. Somehow it felt so different from a year ago. It gets easier to see a whole year at once like that. Well, I've had a lot of practice by now.

And I was reminded again of my friend Joe. I thought of a game we'd officiated together a few years ago, in Olean. There had been a change in the rules that year, an unusual situation arose during the game – both teams wanting to make substitutions at an odd moment, I think – and Joe disallowed something perfectly legal.

You can be certain I let him have it. How could I not? It was the first mistake I could remember him making in twenty-odd years of working together. I did carry on a bit at his expense, no more than was called for, but no less. He shook his head and smiled, and said in that way he had: 'Ja, ja, ja.'

Meaning, 'Oh, do me a favour.'

German words don't always fall nicely on English ears. But it was always a pleasure to hear Joe say that.

And now I'm reminded, in turn, of the only *other* German word I know: *'Nein, nein, nein,'* meaning more or less the same thing, which I learned from a girlfriend during my single days.

I'll keep that story to myself though, I think. That's another way of being grateful for the stories you have. Just holding on to them.

–WJH

Feeling young again

The simple life is best: a nice afternoon walk, a bit of the Premier League on television, church on Sundays, the occasional glass of wine at Dina's. And did you know the year only has two seasons? Indeed it does: soccer season and the offseason, which also goes by the name of 'ski season.' Simpler that way.

And now the offseason's ending. With snow on the ground the village opens to everyone, but every spring the snow melts and green grass peeks through, and it's all ours again for a time. The air feels different. So do I.

I've been frequenting the gym in Springville, oddly enough. One wants to keep trim. That'll do for a winter's day, but it's nothing to running across the field in the sun. One last time for good measure, and that will be enough. Though of course it's never quite enough, is it.

I imagine that up at the school, Mrs Neilon, Mrs Taylor, and Mrs Eddy look forward to it as I do. It's something in the blood, I think. And I know the same goes for Mrs Deb Golley, who keeps the local league humming along steadily. My fair ladies. (I hope they don't mind me saying so.)

I've nothing against springtime romance, mind you, nor summer vacations, nor fall festival. Even your American football will do in a pinch. But I enjoy a simple life, so my year has two seasons; and I can feel them turning.

I hope to see you at the fields this year to share the season with me.

Like looking into a mirror

I was 18 then. Hard to believe. But then, sometimes it's hard to believe a day has passed.

When you're young you spend your birthdays looking forward. Now I tend to look back. I turn 81 this week. 81, 18. That's a lot of life to remember, or even to forget. And to be grateful for.

I remember being expelled from school when I was 15.

And going to Korea and Japan with the army. I arrived as the war was ending. Decent timing.

I remember the Blitz, though I wouldn't mind forgetting.

I remember working in textiles for 11 years in England. Learning what a good suit was, and how to wear one. And much else. Hardly a glamourous job, but then that turned out not to matter a bit.

I can't remember a time that wasn't full up with soccer. If it ever happened, well: better to forget.

You look back and realize all over again how lucky you've been. How many blessings you've received. You wonder how it can possibly hold up. But here you are.

I've visited so many parts of the world, and met so many people. They all stay with you, one way or another. And yet, to finish up here, to be able to work with the kids here in the village, to share the sport I love best with them – that's something special.

I'm so full of gratitude I can't find the words for it.

It's spring. Everything gets to be new again. Even me.

A lot of things get better as you get older. Though not necessarily easier. You let go of so much. You learn to live with pain. But you get to live with so much else as well. And you want to share it all, in a way.

When you're young it's such a thrill to get gifts on your birthday. And then one day it's the other way 'round: having the birthday, and getting to share a little of what you've received, is the gift.

Women's soccer

In my day there was only one women's football team in England – and they played against men's teams, in exhibition matches.

But this week I watched Germany and Norway draw 1-1 in the World Cup. The pitch (and sidelines, and the stands!) were swarming with beautiful women. The football was superb.

And – it's strange to say this, believe me – the US team are the favourites to win the World Cup.

I'm grateful for the chance to watch the world change.

This country came from nearly nothing as far as soccer goes, you know. Many of the top coaches at the Women's World Cup are men, and worked in men's soccer first. But here in the US there are so many talented women coaches with years and years of experience – at every level. They had to learn so much so fast, and they did.

If you like, you can go watch the ECS team to see what that a coach with that kind of experience is capable of.

The news on the TV is rarely good, lately – and there's an awful lot of it. But I watch the US women play, and I remember what this country is capable of. You can be so organized and committed, so patient, when you're building something that's meant to last for generations.

Everything changes. Arsenal, one of the best teams in the Premier League, recently fielded a side without a single Englishman.

Well. There's an midfielder named Williams. She's played for England since she was a teenager and has more caps than any other Englishwoman. For her first few years on the national team, she was homeless. She wouldn't tell her teammates. You can watch her play in Canada this week. If England beat Columbia, you can watch her next week too.

Everything changes, and things have always been complicated. As always, though, there's much to be proud of, and much to look forward to.

Best,

Wally Holland Sr.

A delightful result

The final games of each baseball season in America are called the "World Series," but only American teams (and the Toronto Blue Jays) actually play in it. Many people in other countries find it a bit silly.

But no one laughs about a World Cup win.

And today we have one. Something to be proud of.

The newspapers say 30 million Americans watched the end of the final against Japan. (Our team won, 5-2.) That's something to be proud of as well. It's a wonderful feeling, cheering for your countrymen. Seeing how much hard work goes into it.

The American men's team has never gotten past the semifinals, and that was in 1930 – before I was born, if you can believe that. Catching up is a hard job, and they're improving.

This was a special win. What prevailed above all is good tidings, kindred spirits. The way the women's players carry themselves and each other, they seem like good human beings. Look at the dignity of the Japanese and German teams as they were beaten. That's a hard thing, you know.

The head of the American men's team is a German, Jürgen Klinsmann, a superb player when he was younger. He used to coach Bayern Munich. The women's coach is an Englishwoman named Jill Ellis, who never had a chance to play on a proper team as a girl. There were no English girls' leagues in those days.

She finally got to play when she was 15 – after moving to the United States. It's funny, in a way.

I have to tell you, I didn't like seeing England lose. They were the better side against Japan. That's life though. And I'll say this. I didn't mind seeing them beat Germany. An Englishwoman named Fara Williams scored the winning goal. For her first six years playing for England, she was homeless. Now she has more caps than any other English player. You can't keep these women down.

We have that same spirit in Ellicottville. I can't believe it sometimes. World Cup victories start in places like our village, with kids and coaches and communities like ours.

As I often do, I think of my friends Joe and Adam Delity. I remember when there was no boys' team in the village. It may seem like a small thing, to have a soccer team in a little town in the country. But to me it isn't.

Soccer wasn't born here but it grows here. It's found a home here. That means the world to someone like me. After all, I wasn't born here either.

I like to think I can do justice to the game I love, and the kids who play it. And to my friends. The work they started here. It goes on, quietly. Something wonderful grows here, a little at a time. Once in a while you get a victory like this week's. And it keeps growing.

What could be more American than that?

End of season pride

My eldest son, in one of his books, quoted these words from a man named Oscar Ichazo: 'No one is truly sane until he feels gratitude toward the whole universe.'

I must say, I've felt myself going a bit mad at times. Haven't we all? But I know what he means.

Time passes, life gets better and worse, and you find yourself wanting to give thanks every time you wake up.

The fall soccer season ended. I did 30 games in seven weeks. At 81 years old I feel a bit of pride at that number. And do you know – I feel as good as I have in years. My knee's bad, my heart isn't a young man's heart.

But a young man's heart isn't full the way mine is.

My last game of the season was at Ellicottville, which is always nice. The boys modified team – they won, deservedly so. They're a wonderful team. Some superb individual players on the team, and they play *smart*, with real skill.

An official can't root for one team over another, of course. But I was proud of our boys.

When I was a teenager I was less than five feet tall. I was going to be a jockey. I wasn't sad to grow out of it, I must say. The modified boys are small like I was. I have to admit: a few of them could've outplayed me, back then. They play a superior game to the one I knew.

Afterward I had to walk across the field where the varsity team was playing. It was pouring rain. Katie Karassik walked up and gave me a proper kiss on the lips. All I could think was: 'I'm *freezing!* Don't let go!'

Sometimes kids approach me on the street, 8 or 10 years old, and say hi. They recognize me from the games. That feeling, you can't put a price on it. My boys live in other cities with families of their own, my wife passed on long ago, but I never feel isolated or old here.

It's strange to say, but I feel *excited* lately. That last game at the school in town, it felt a bit like the last cheer of the World Cup. Like the start of something.

As I boy I lived 300 yards from Georgie Best. Watching him play was the climax of all the soccer I've seen in life. But here, now, watching our own kids playing at the school, I get another feeling. Endurance. They lift me up.

They pay me too much to do this job. I should be paying them. (Mind you, I'll still cash the checks, thanks.)

To the parents and grandparents who come watch our game every week: from the bottom of my heart, thank you. See you next season.

–Wally Holland, Sr.

Indoor soccer

You're never too old to make a beginner mistake.

I'm pleased – overjoyed, really – to report this good news firsthand, from recent experience.

I refereed my first game of indoor soccer last Saturday at the new sports complex in Salamanca: 17-year-old boys and girls playing 35-minute matches. It's a smashing building, by the way. A nice thing for their community. They need something like that, and deserve it.

The summer season's coming up – a lot of kids came over to say hi. And indoor soccer is soccer, after all. The ball is round and so forth. But that's as familiar as it got.

It was a revelation. The pace, the strategy.

And I found myself making a big mistake at one point. I've been an official for a long, long time. But in the gym, it was a funny thing: I didn't know where to position myself. I ended up too close to the wall, was caught in the middle of the play, got turned around.

On the field, you know, I'd have known what to do without thinking about it.

The younger officials were even more efficient than me.

All the same it was a wonderful feeling. I turn 82 years old in a few weeks, and here I was, doing something new. Learning.

The snow's gone. The season's coming. I passed my travel league federation test, and have been getting physically ready. My friend Ray Johnson asked me to do the indoor games. They have a wonderful organization, the indoor officials – competitive to get into. There's a fresh feeling there.

I was a bit embarrassed at the game. But I was proud and happy afterward to have made a beginner mistake. It means I'm at the start of something new.

July 2016

Summer's begun.

To clarify, I mean 'summer soccer' of course. But I suppose you knew that.

It's a new season with new faces, on the field and off. Lindsey Coburn is in charge now, doing fine work, along with Catlin Toth, Katie Mendel, Lianna Olsen – and some gentlemen. There's no point naming *them*, we'll be here all day.

I see last year's 6-year-olds turning up as remarkable little 7-year-old players. What a difference a year makes. Summer is for watching things grow and change.

The young girls are showing real promise. I think it helps that they've grown up seeing older sisters and friends do so well at Ellicottville school. But there's a different sort of pride as well.

Their team, our team, won the World Cup after all. In the American way.

We used to get perhaps 50 people coming to our games. Now we'll see 75 or more. People stop me on the street wanting to talk, enthusiastic, people you'd never *believe* would want to talk about soccer.

I remember living in Texas in 1982, talking about soccer and having no one know what the hell I was talking about. Now I'll meet parents in Ellicottville who know what 'FIFA' stands for. Incredible.

The news seems dark all the time and this is a small thing, only a bit of light. But I suppose that's enough to see where you're going.

School soccer is months away. We officials will meet beforehand to prepare for the season. I hope to be fit and ready for the season, though my knee will have the final say. By way of contribution to the league, I've cut down to one or two glasses of wine a week, and a daily trip to the gym. The wine was the greater sacrifice.

I've been in America 38 years and feel more American than English, these days. I can't imagine living anywhere but our village. Lately I feel like I live in two worlds: the reality of getting older, little by little – and then, everywhere I look, such beauty.

My Cata

I was home again today,
Started to look around the room
My thoughts covered miles of ground
Lately they go that way, thinking of my problems
There's fear overlooking my assets so dear
I read Wally's poem, Phillippe's too
Then I remembered thinking mostly of you
You weather my anger, my despair
Verbal abuse rides in the air
You always cook my meal
No matter when or how you feel
So thinking now, shouting out loud
Why do I feel so very proud
It's not that I give, the way I live
But we are proud parents of two smart kids
We will never ask God for more
In unison we have, we both adore
Two wonderful, no longer little boys
Years flash past, they remain joys
And we will always love them both
For you, always my betrothed

Ellicottville
1993

Acknowledgments

This book has taken a long time to write, and it could not have been written without a lot of help. I'm very grateful to the following people for making this book possible:

Lynn Timon; the irreplaceable Laura Flanagan at the Ellicottville library; Bob McCarthy; Gary and Marie at Spring Creek Gym; the staff at Katie's; Mark Ward; Kathy and Jim Illig; Dr Pfalzer and Fran; the staff at Dina's; Dina DiPasquale and Jim Carls; the fellows at the American Legion; the Telaak family; the folks at Red Apple and Tops markets; the staff at Five Star Bank; Katie Karassik and John Karassik; Sam Wilson at *Salamanca Press*; Golley's Garage; John Thomas at the *Villager*; Sir Nick Pitillo; the Ellicottville Brewery; Holiday Valley; the staff of the Beef and Barrel restaurant in Olean; Springville Library; American Store in Ellicottville; the Springville Center for the Arts; Jennie Acklin and Alicia Dziak at the Ellicottville and Springville *Times* papers; John Ash of Olean; Susan and Vera at Anything Printed, Katy and Victor Katy's Cafe; Bruce Fashion Arts; Finnerty's Tap Room; Madigan's.

To anyone I've forgotten: forgive me, and thank you.

My son Phillippe spent hours going over the manuscript with his brother Wally to make sure it wasn't 'embarrassing' or 'grossly inaccurate.' Wally has been working on this book for years, along with me. I'm so grateful to them.

This book is dedicated to my wife, Kathleen.

ABOUT THE AUTHORS

Walter Holland Sr lives in Ellicottville NY.
This is his first book.
He can be reached at *wallyholland@yahoo.com*.

Walter Holland Jr lives in Cambridge MA.
He has written several books, fiction and non-,
He can be reached at *wgh@alum.mit.edu*,
and on Twitter as *@waxbanks*.

Printed in Great Britain
by Amazon